NEW CLASS CULTURE

How an Emergent Class Is Transforming America's Culture

Avrom Fleishman

PRAEGER

Westport, Connecticut
London

Library of Congress Cataloging-in-Publication Data

Fleishman, Avrom.
New class culture : how an emergent class is transforming America's culture /
Avrom Fleishman.
p. cm.
Includes bibliographical references and index.
ISBN 0–275–97777–3 (alk. paper)
1. Elite (Social sciences)—United States. 2. Social classes—United States. 3. High
technology—Social aspects—United States. 4. Social change—United States.
5. Popular culture—United States. 6. United States—Social conditions—1980–
I. Title.
HN90.E4 F54 2002
305.5'0973—dc21 2002025307

British Library Cataloguing in Publication Data is available.

Library of Congress Catalog Card Number: 2002025307
ISBN: 0–275–97777–3

First published in 2002

Praeger Publishers, 88 Post Road West, Westport, CT 06881
An imprint of Greenwood Publishing Group, Inc.
www.praeger.com

Printed in the United States of America

The paper used in this book complies with the
Permanent Paper Standard issued by the National
Information Standards Organization (Z39.48–1984).

10 9 8 7 6 5 4 3 2 1

For Saskia

O my America!
my new-found land.
—John Donne

Contents

Preface

A new class is always a source of emergent cultural practice, but while it is still, as a class, relatively subordinate, this is always likely to be uneven and is certain to be incomplete.
                                                    —Raymond Williams

Every society has its culture, but only specially favored nations enjoy the luxury of arguing about it. Anthropologists tell us that tribal culture stabilizes and unifies individual and collective life, for customary practices and traditional meanings are ordering, even binding, forces. In contrast, culture in technologically advanced and developing societies becomes a focus of controversy surrounding new patterns in work and consumption. By the same token, such changes are registered in and may most readily be grasped by examining the culture and its controversies. Beyond expressing both exhilaration and resistance to change, our culture wars—for all their excess of heat over light—are signs of deeper change. They serve as indices of social regrouping, as an information economy brings into existence a new kind of worker—sometimes called "knowledge workers"—to run it and, in doing so, reorders the structure of society by adding a potent new stratum to it.

In a nation as ideologically fissured as ours, it may be cause for rejoicing when agreement on any basic issue is reached. Both right and left acknowledge that a new social group—a creature of many names, given its newness and the variety of attitudes to it—is both politically suspect and morally dubious. Starting in the seventies, neoconservatives have decried the survival of the radical sixties virus among the now grown-up ex-student protesters. Both the apathetic relativism of young professionals, once derisively labeled as yuppies, and the would-be radicalism of the politically correct on the campuses have been tarred with the same brush—at times using the sociologists' term, "New Class," with heavy irony. These sometimes well-justified exposés of dangerous political naïveté have been matched by left-wing condemnation—ostensibly political but fundamentally ethical—of the rise of "narcissism" or consumer excess among the newly well-heeled. Although many recognize that this new social group is no passing phenomenon of quirky trendiness but has become a rooted presence on the American scene, there exists a deep suspicion of its current and potential influence.

A jaundiced eye is cast both by journalists who follow the working lives and opinions of the new technologists and by observers who profess to be sympathetic members of that same set. Whereas Paulina Borsook's title *Cyberselfish: A Critical Romp Through the Terribly Libertarian Culture of High Tech* (2000) tells exactly where she stands, David Brooks's *Bobos in Paradise: The New Upper Class and How They Got There* (2000) is more ambivalent. Much of the book is devoted to sharply observed satire of the ecological correctness and nostalgic taste of these bourgeois bohemians (or is it bohemian bourgeois?), yet it closes by honoring their mellow social tolerance and relative indifference to the culture wars. Despite Brooks's effort to get beyond the fulminations of his neoconservative mentors against what they viewed as New Class radicalism (he instead labels this temperament "conservative" in a broader-than-political sense), he depicts a vaguely left-leaning intelligentsia for whom those who "fall outside the ranks of Bobo respectability" are invariably men of money and right-wing power. Meanwhile Borsook shows the high-tech elements of this group to be primitive-capitalist in their competitive behavior and antigovernment attitudes. What has this still emerging and thus somewhat inarticulate grouping done to deserve such negative or contradictory ratings?

Although answers to this question will emerge in this book, it is already evident that criticism of the New Class offers tacit acknowledgment of a fact about turn-of-the-millennium America usually ignored or denied: that it is a class society. Social transformation in the wake of high technology has, moreover, tended not toward classlessness but toward the formation of new classes, with the inevitable tensions that new entrants generate. (The underclass, those effectively excluded from regular employment in a high-tech economy, is the other chief example of social tensions surrounding a new stratum.) Suspicions about knowledge workers may well be felt by those who own and ultimately, if not operationally, control the industries and institutions these specialists serve.

Many of these specialists become, of course, substantial proprietors themselves, while usually maintaining their technical orientation. In addition, resentment of this new breed of white-collar worker by the manual working class is only to be expected when the former becomes palpably influential in an economy where the latter's jobs are threatened and often eliminated. Political and ethical disdain of the New Class may be traced to understandable anxieties in both the mega-propertied and working classes (or at least in their appointed or self-appointed spokesmen), for they stand at points of engagement but also friction with it.

Our culture wars may, in turn, be seen as the continuation of social and economic rivalries by other means. But if these controversies limn the structure of a society in transformation, what can be said of the culture itself—considered not as a congeries of performances and artifacts but as a functional system? This study assumes that the premises that guide literary, art, and other historians in treating past cultural phenomena are operative for characterizing contemporary America as well. Just as Renaissance or Victorian culture conveyed in complex and subtle (as well as not so subtle) ways the rise, at different stages, of a new dominant class, the emergence of a new, potentially dominant class is registered in contemporary, often called "postmodern," culture. These interpretive premises may be acted on well or badly, with the dogmatics of Marxist theory or the sensitivity of a Meyer Schapiro or a Simon Schama, but it seems merely obscurantist to maintain that class-cultural analysis is irrelevant to contemporary America, as if it were a classless society.

There is, to be sure, an alternative sociocultural view of America that is widely shared in both learned and unlearned circles. It is the view that since America is a polyethnic society (to use a term more neutral than the now heavily freighted "multicultural"), its culture is polyethnic, too. From this it is sometimes made to follow that the class configuration of our culture, if not entirely nugatory, is secondary to the ethnic. There's no denying the relevance to our culture of ethnic awareness, yet some of the baggage it carries may require special handling. Other nations have or have had polyethnic societies—ancient Rome, India, most Moslem lands—their stability based on assigning distinct economic roles to the various ethnicities, in effect turning them into functional classes. (William McNeill's *Polyethnicity and National Unity in World History* is the master text here; Bernard Lewis's studies of the Islamic world supply copious data.) Although ethnic class assignment in the United States has become considerably more complicated than it was under slavery or with earlier mass immigration, large segments of ethnic groups perform, with often attractive variations, according to the norms of one or another class.

Since the nation's consciousness has for decades been preoccupied with redressing the grievances of minority groups, it has come to be assumed that ethnic differences stand not only at the origin but at the end of the process by which people's life chances are determined. Yet although ethnicity continues to direct large numbers of, for example, border-state Latinos toward established economic roles, their workaday lives and daily experiences in a mass marketing system make for a culture common to them and to non-Latino workers, which can only be called lower- or working-class culture, ethnically inflected. Social scientists can fruitfully show the complexity and variance of lower-class behavior by region, ethnicity, and other factors. Yet purveyors and advertisers of consumer goods, fabricators of television and musical entertainment, designers of fast-food outlets, and recreational facilities have no difficulty regarding this as a fairly homogeneous audience at the low end of the mass market. (They also, to be sure, shrewdly craft messages and products toward segments of the working class, as sitcoms with primarily black audiences and Spanish-language broadcasting attest.)

Another and related inattention operates in current cultural discourse: just as it would be vaguely "racist" to speak of better or worse ethnic contributions to the common culture, it is now insufferably snobbish to suggest that "mass"—now called "popular"—culture is at all inferior to "high"—now called "elite"—culture, or that middle-class culture has anything to apologize for. The shifting in the terms themselves conveys the ideological element of such discussions: they convey not only a tacit acknowledgment of classes—"upper" and "lower" and in between—and the correlation of cultural goods with them, but a form of resistance to the mere idea of social as well as cultural hierarchy. The prevailing temper regards the existence of class divisions as an embarrassment, if not an injustice, and esthetic judgments based on them as an affront. I shall use the term "populist" for views conveying these sentiments, though I trust not with excessive distortion despite their variety and frequent murkiness.

With all the elevated thinking of current populists, who stand in a long and honorable tradition not only in the farmers' and workers' movements but in American intellectual history as well, it must be said that they are beating a live horse. People continue to value and select markedly different objects and experiences not randomly or with total independence of their social circumstances, but with observable tendencies according to their class standing. Nor, despite their functional value in satisfying differing needs, are these selections immune to esthetic judgments. Even Pierre Bourdieu's *Distinction*, the sociological text most often cited to underwrite the populist challenge to hierarchical distinctions, denotes the culture of the upper and better-educated classes as "legitimate" taste. Only in America can it be maintained that, although unique works of art suffused with the aura of individual artists are auctioned before eager buyers for figures approaching a hundred million dollars, there is no qualitative difference between a fine art and a mass cultural object. (The quality/reward ratio is, admittedly, a tricky ground for argument, since some pop music discs and action films also reap astronomic returns, though by different marketing routes.)

To avoid what must surely become fruitless normative criticism, given the ideological loading of all positions in the "high/low" debate, I shall pursue another, yet related, thesis: that the main trends in American culture, or at least in cultural discourse, have been given their present form by the emergence of a new class, which adds its mite to the social forces that shape, if not determine, class cultures. This nation's culture in the twentieth century was largely derived from the mass production and marketing programs of a developed industrial system, while retaining specialized fabrication and distribution routes for distinct groups within it. This regime of production and consumption spews out manufactured and media products with apparently universal appeal while carefully generating varieties designed to satisfy the special tastes of different classes. By century's end and for the foreseeable future this offering in consumption and culture was and will be elaborated to appeal to a new social element, the New Class.

To make these propositions plausible, I argue in an opening chapter that the long-standing populist view of American culture is at best a limited and largely a wishful one, expressing fervid hopes for equality rather than facing up to the cultural consequences of class division. The chapter that follows summarizes the views of Bourdieu and other sociologists that not only culture but cultural discourse is distributed by class, so that even the arts community's arguments for cultural democracy can be seen to carry heavy class burdens. To illustrate the current structure of this discourse, I cite a gathering of arts professionals conducted by the National Endowment for the Arts. In another chapter setting the scene, I inquire into a condition in which America may genuinely be said to be exceptional: the prevailing avoidance of class recognition in American cultural thinking, matched by a touching confusion about class standing among the general public as well. The effect of recognizing that every class has its culture is to bring light and air to the normative struggles and avoidances in the high/low, modern/postmodern, and other contentions.

The chapters that follow focus on the New Class itself. The first of these attempts to characterize the modes of thought and behavior that make this group distinctive—although, in line with its diverse social origins, its cultural inclinations range more widely than the fixed levels sought out by other classes. Another chapter isolates elements of the culture that mark the New Class's interests and desires, and estimates the degree to which these artifacts and activities fulfill their promise for these patrons. Although the New Class's taste may strike one as omnivorous, there are signs that its cultural participation is not an openly inclusive but a searchingly selective process, for which the leading figures in cultural production and criticism are fulfilling their guidance functions with only limited success. A final chapter indulges in speculation on the New Class's prospects for broadening its perspective beyond trendy multicultural awareness, to a worldwide and worldly scale, in which it might become a bellwether for the society at large. The unintended outcome of this class's heterogeneous ethnic origins and global informational reach may be a new variety of cosmopolitanism, in which rational hope can be invested for America's cultural growth and social health.

* * *

These aims would not have come as close to fulfillment as they have without the ministrations of the following loyal friends: Joel Belson, Felicia Bonaparte, Milton Cummings, Reed Dasenbrock, James Goodwin, Robert Gordon, John Higham, and Ross Posnock. Their advice on matters of style, fact, and opinion has been followed only as capacity and inclination permit, hence their surviving innocence.

The dedication carries personal but also representative significance. As the maternal descendant of a great American and the paternal descendant of more recent immigrants, my granddaughter manifests the melting pot in her own person and comes equipped with ample material and cultural resources to wisely inherit the future.

1

Our Cultures and Our Classes

Here lie the archives of Eden.

—George Steiner

Culture talk usually begins by raising leading questions, but instead of arguing about what culture is or whose culture it is, we might ask, Where is culture to be found? As is generally recognized, culture is a process or performance at a number of mental, interpersonal, and collective levels, yet the artifacts involved in those activities have a durable existence that lends itself to collection and display, whether for tribal use and veneration or for scientific and esthetic inspection. As anthropologists and art historians often point out, museums place these items outside their functional context and thereby obscure or distort them, yet we remain devoted museum-goers for all that. If a busy tourist felt compelled to learn about American culture on the fly, he could do worse than making the rounds of Washington's Mall or New York's "museum mile," though more personal contacts and mature understanding might come later.

Other nations have their culture quarters: Berlin's *Museumsinsel* and other complexes, London's South Kensington, and Paris's Seine banks testify to the convenient clustering and cumulative impressiveness of such agglomerations. Even more than they, America's museums manifest the many-sidedness of a national culture, ranging from fine arts to popular media, from history to science and technology, with ethnic, gender, and other special contributions prominent, often in institutions or wings of their own. American culture may be variously depicted (in a discourse to be inspected below), but it is forcibly made present to the mind in these sumptuous monuments. The irritable notion—developed in the wake of inconsistent federal support for artists and performance groups—that "the United States has never had a national cultural policy" strangely overlooks the palpable presence of federal museums, archives, libraries, arboretums, zoos, theaters, protected historic sites, and so on, staffed by innumerable specialists in these fields and providing invaluable sustenance to its citizenry.[1]

There may not be a unitary American culture but there's much culture in America, drawn, like the nation's population itself, from worldwide sources and, in line with our social structure's distribution, spanning the full range of taste. Given the vast and growing museum attendance figures, Americans (and visitors) of all class and ethnic stripes seem to be adventuring beyond their constricted initial positions. Not only from museum to museum but even within a single one, the culture's many-sidedness may be recognized. The turn-of-millennium *American Century* shows at the Whitney Museum of American Art displayed the full gamut of works that might conceivably be honored as culture, from abstract paintings to industrial products, in media ranging from literature to cinema and electronics. Just as "diversity" has become a mantra in social relations and education, inclusiveness distinguishes the American approach to culture, although other nations have made halting steps in this direction.

With the rise of the term "culture" in the national discourse—magnified by its barbed usage in political debates on ethical and social concerns—the term "art" has lost its honorific sense. When works in all media or with any function may be accepted as art, the category overlaps that of culture, and the latter term becomes the operative one. The country may or may not be producing good art, but everything it does is American culture. Insofar as culture is an anthropological concept, there seems little point in rendering esthetic judgment on its products if they work well within a social system any more than there would be in judging Balinese cockfighting or the Virgin of Guadalupe cult on esthetic grounds alone. Yet anthropologists, like many a layman, recognize that these practices have an esthetic dimension that is not irrelevant to their social functions.

Although both public and specialist opinions tend toward an inclusive view of culture, certain features of the scene present openings for the worm of division. Just as a nation whose creed is equality and inclusion is still riven, as throughout its history, by inequality and contestation, so that nation's culture exhibits the diverse tastes of classes and groups existing side by side with scant mutual comprehension or sympathy. To visit a vast storehouse of artifacts such as the National Museum of American History in Washington or the Shelburne Museum in Vermont is to be forcibly impressed by the variety of American arts and the myriad sources of their inspiration. Yet the shock of multitudinousness cannot override another powerful impression: the clear separation of objects, reflecting different life practices. At the Shelburne, the fine art collection is housed in its own building, displaying the exclusive lifestyle of even these eclectic and sympathetic collectors of vernacular objects. On a grander scale, the government has established distinct museums for the fine arts and for the objects of work and play: the National Gallery of Art and the American History museum, respectively. These separations are attributable neither to the donors' snobbery nor the curators' convenience alone, for they speak to another American reality that stands out as clearly here as at other culture islands. We see collections of objects that people of different classes used and valued: Toby jugs and Oriental porcelain, election posters and antique coins, sheet music and opera programs, the work of itinerant portraitists and Beaux Art sculpture, as varied tastes have acquired, employed, and valued them. American culture has been and remains a host of class cultures.

In response to this dazzling array, commentators of assorted hues have celebrated its ethnic, regional, and other contributors but, in keeping with a habitual reticence, rarely its class divisions. The determined amnesia that makes class an objectionable consideration in political and social discourse extends to culture talk. Even a recent characterization of our culture by a doyen of the field, notable for his companionable tolerance, maintains this omission. "When a kaleidoscope is in motion," writes Lawrence H. Fuchs, "the parts give the appearance of rapid change and extensive variety in color and shape and in their interrelationships."[2] This metaphor, while it stresses a wholesome interaction among ethnic constituents and their fluid transitions over time, bears subtle features that suggest another side of its tenor (the culture). Like the images of a kaleidoscope, the patterns of American culture are indeed manifold, yet they display not only changefulness but crystalline regularity. National, like tribal, cultures each have a detectable structure derived from the form of the society in which they are generated. In America, as elsewhere and at other times, this latter is a class structure, constantly changing indeed yet fairly stable as a system over time. Still, the idea that there are bourgeois or working-class cultures in America has come to seem an alien notion, although weaker terms such as "middle-class culture" are sometimes employed. Upper-class taste is, however, singled out for ideological attack in such sobriquets as "elite culture," so that class division in the cultural realm has not been entirely abandoned, merely given selective attention.

Although they're designed to avoid bringing class directly into discussion, the terms long used in cultural discourse are freighted with signs of its presence. The class hostility shrouded by intellectual contempt in Dwight Macdonald's famous definition is patent enough: "High Culture—that is chronicled in the textbooks, and a novel kind that is manufactured for the market. This latter may be called Mass Culture, or better Masscult, since it really isn't culture at all."[3] Equally class oriented, though more evocative of the qualities of their object, are the sociologist Edward Shils's terms for middle- and lower-class cultures: "mediocre" and "brutal," respectively.[4] The same normativity is present in the once popular hierarchy of terms—highbrow, middlebrow, lowbrow—aligned with the common terms for class hierarchy.[5] Cultural discourse would more closely approach cultural reality if it were attentive to class-related pursuits and preferences; it would also profit from a clear-cut terminology that recognized these facts without subtle expressions of personal taste or class animosity.

* * *

When cultural historians pay attention to class distinctions, they usually do so only to deplore them. The strongest recent view on class and culture in American history may be called the "sacralization" thesis, after its defining negative note. The notion sketched by the sociologist Paul J. DiMaggio and developed by historian Lawrence W. Levine that America once had a unified culture—when Shakespeare was enjoyed by the masses and elites danced the Virginia reel—but suffered a fall from grace through a turn-of-the-century "sacralization" of high culture follows the pattern of other myths of the Fall.[6] Class, as much as race and ethnicity, has long made our fractious nation a place of permeable but distinct cultures.

The "sacralization" thesis links two propositions that, although reflecting a truth, hardly tell the whole story. The first, that antebellum America enjoyed a "promiscuous combination of genres that would later be considered incompatible" (DiMaggio, p. 43), has an obvious plausibility, on the evidence of musical evenings ranging from symphony and opera to fanfare and ballad, or theatrical programs including both Shakespeare or Dickens and gymnasts or contortionists. But these studies themselves take note that high cultural organizations such as Boston's Handel and Haydn Society and Philharmonic Society arose well before the purported end-of-century separation, that is, that they were associated with post–Civil War developments in industry and urbanization. The motivations of both earlier and later culture promoters were considerably more complex than the dichotomy between promiscuous mixing and exclusive separation proclaims. Early museums' mingling of fine art with a plethora of attractions such as natural history and folk art were, as at the

Peale museums in Baltimore and Philadelphia, nets to catch a wider audience than those devoted to the family's refined paintings. Enlarging the variety of exhibits to increase the potential market thus served to juxtapose high and low culture, but it built on taste differences already differentiated by class.

Moreover, what is taken to be the easy mingling of low with high culture may actually represent more elevated tastes than those that have been suggested. Levine (p. 147) construes Charles Wilson Peale's exhibition of a mastodon skeleton and other natural curiosities as a sign of mixed taste levels; it may be more to the point that his organizing of the mastodon's exhumation—commemorated proudly in his once famous painting of the scene—along with his other scientific activities indicate a growing personal and national intellectual curiosity, so that the Peale museums may stand not only as America's first art but also its first science museums.[7]

Even when the broad contrast between pre– and post–Civil War culture is granted, it must also be acknowledged that the vaunted unified culture, to the extent it existed, was a constant subject of embarrassment and proposed uplifting by intellectuals who are our culture's seminal figures, not merely its elitist snobs. For a more intimate sense of the earlier culture, one might apply to such novelists as Mark Twain, whose portrait in *Huckleberry Finn* of the king and the duke as purveyors of Shakespeare ("To be or not to be, with a bare bodkin") rings truer than current accounts of popular reception of the classics. What is accounted a fall from grace by present-day populists may well have seemed a redemption from naiveté and ignorance by intellectuals of a society still in the early stages of nation building.

A second proposition holds that the founding of museums, opera houses, and so on was a program by "cultural capitalists" to separate themselves from the threatening masses, devising nonprofit institutions "that could claim to serve the community, even as they defined the community to include only the elite and the upper-middle classes" (DiMaggio, p. 47). Steven Conn's *Museums and American Intellectual Life, 1876–1926* shows, however, that the intentions for the Philadelphia Museum of Art and Boston Museum of Fine Arts "were precisely not to be palaces of fine art but functional places instead where art would be put to the service of industry," including schools for the vocational training of working people.[8] When sumptuous private collections of fine art were acquired, museum attendance went steeply up, and the provision of free entrance days from the outset made these hallowed halls accessible to the full community. An uplifting impulse no doubt existed among the patrons of these institutions, but their patronizing tone should not dispel appreciation of their progressive educational aims. When opprobrium is dealt out, the "sacralization" thesis studiously avoids considering the parallel formation of what has come to be called the mass culture industry, which made the formation of lower- and middle-class tastes as narrow and self-assertive as those ascribed to the "cultural capitalists."

The term employed for such processes as "sacralization" by scholars on the left is "hegemony": the creation and employment of cultural institutions—like what has been called the "Institutional State Apparatuses" of family, church, school, et cetera—to sustain the dominant classes in their domination. Some such development was to be expected in the later nineteenth century, the heyday of high capitalism, with the attendant crystallization of both capitalist and working classes in a period of keen industrial conflict. In this context, the "sacralization" thesis refers in an oblique fashion to the flowering of distinctive cultures to serve the emergent classes. By ignoring the normal cultural consequences of class formation, in its tone of revelatory muckraking of elitist impositions on the body politic, it stands strong in the populist tradition. American populism is no doubt primarily a political phenomenon, as its latest historian insists, but it is also active in the long train of celebrations of the people's culture, with reciprocal devaluation of high culture.[9]

Again, it takes a novelist, like one of our contemporaries, E. Annie Proulx, to undercut the sentimentality suffusing latter-day populism: her novel *Accordion Crimes* conveys a visceral sense of ethnic violence and class animosity in the turn-of-the-century circulation of cultural goods (in this case, an accordion). Moreover, divisive impulses have, as pop culture critics know, been unleashed as much from below in the social hierarchy as from above—indeed, that is why the more radical among them value pop so highly.[10] With its visible and in some cases avowed political bias, patronizing toward the lower classes and bitter against the upper, the populist strain in culture criticism stands in that venerable American tradition, anti-intellectualism. This impulse, almost as prevalent in the intelligentsia as in other groups, has always targeted its class animus at elegant tastes as well as difficult ideas. The class conflicts that invigorate culture talk are nowhere as palpable as in the populist discourse, historical and current, that hopes to minimize class distinctions and uphold a culture for all.

A truly democratic orientation toward the "cultural capitalists" would regard their contributions with less suspicion than is the current predisposition. Capitalist provisions of the finer things to those without money persist to the present day, as witnessed by J. Paul Getty's stipulation that no admission fee be charged at his museums, a policy made possible by the largesse of his endowments. And their educative influence continues to be felt, as the variety as well as quantity of visitors to high-culture emporia grows. Irrespective of the extent to which the lower classes actually enjoy such resources, their value to the nation as testifying to a collective aspiration toward the good, true, and beautiful will be doubted only by those confirmed in deconstructive skepticism of such values.

The populist charge against the upper class goes beyond undercutting its efforts to spread its wealth of acquisitions and move by this channel toward a shared culture. The charge takes the resentful tack of denigrating the "finer things" as no better than or—because "socially constructed" for ideological purposes—no different from the works of the people. In its effort to bring down the mighty in art and power, the tribunes of the people exhibit a less inclusive spirit than that displayed by many of their targets. The upper orders have not always held themselves superior to popular achievements. Although the great Medicis such as Morgan and Walters were exclusively focused on high culture (though in a multicultural variety), others such as Electra Havemeyer Webb and Beatrice Chrysler Garbisch were collecting the folk as well as the fine arts with a like devotion and sympathy. They just didn't put them in the same place, either in their homes—to judge by the Shelburne's distribution—or in museums. (The National Gallery now holds the latter's collection of vernacular paintings, displaying its homespun glories in a separate suite of rooms.) It is, indeed, largely through the efforts of such grande dames that folk or vernacular arts have been made accessible to today's omnivorous museum-goers.

Just as museums enshrine the several class cultures, American literature exhibits the ways in which class identities color ethnic and racial conflicts. From Hawthorne to Faulkner, in Wharton as keenly as in Norris, class distinctions produce not only character but destiny. It is remarkable that American Studies, a scholarly field lately invigorated by a version of social-context analysis called the New Historicism, has largely remained innocent of the idea that America's is a set of class cultures. The standard view is that the class struggle "does not form an important part of [the major authors'] outlook."[11] "Class struggle" is probably rejected here for its Marxist overtones, but the term may be used more flexibly to cover the culture wars played out in works from *The House of the Seven Gables* to Don DeLillo's *Underworld*.

Current avoidance of class distinctions in literary critical discourse was to be expected, since a long tradition of intellectual reflection on America's culture has been directed toward overcoming hierarchy and celebrating the masses and their arts. As Emerson delicately put it in "The American Scholar," democratic intellectuals should aim at "the elevation of what is called the lowest classes," and their program has been Whitman's "program of culture . . . not for a single class alone." In our own time, as in the nineteenth century, the myth of a once or future classless culture has been generated to avoid or deplore the fact of taste distinctions, which leads some people's preferences to be held inferior to others'. Seen in historical perspective, the campaign for greater national investment in the arts represents the latest phase in a long-standing struggle by a liberal intelligentsia on behalf of lower-class aspirations to cultural legitimacy—with complementary asperity toward elite culture and intellectual snobbery.

It is rare to find an American Studies expert who, like Leo Marx, will describe the discourse of American letters as "a kind of class struggle," in which one wing, the dominant one among intellectuals, has long aimed to authorize and create a "vernacular ethos [of] radical egalitarianism."[12] Marx's summary view is that, although "many of our most gifted writers have been committed to it, . . . in varying degrees they all have been compelled to recognize America's failure to develop a vernacular culture." This puts the issue too severely, for it is undeniable that groups in the lower classes have created cultural resources after their own tastes and needs, but Marx is addressing the larger claims or aspirations of populist intellectuals. For all Whitman's rhetoric of a unified future in "Democratic Vistas" and despite his lifelong efforts to inspire and exemplify a quasi-popular poetic style, he chafed at the abiding fact that "a scornful superciliousness rules in literature." Well into the new century, George Santayana found the "genteel tradition" continuing to dominate the cultural scene. And so it largely remained.

At the end of the twentieth century, with all the blending of stylistic registers in pop and related art and literary movements, and for all the continued deploring of "high/low," "fine art/popular art" distinctions, the differentiation of audiences and the means employed to reach them still obtained. The great institutions—the Metropolitan and a few comparable museums, the Metropolitan Opera, the half-dozen world-class symphony orchestras—are now surrounded by a host of new and revived institutions around the country, and are disproportionately subvented not only by the rich and nouveau riche but by foundations dedicated to the people at large, including the National Endowment for the Arts. At the same time as popular arts and media have flourished, with handsome commercial and philanthropic support, high culture retains its prestige and even extends its following among other classes without lessening its distinctiveness. Class division remains the norm for American culture, as it does in American society, and the failure to transcend it helps account for the continued intellectual campaign to reject categorization and emphasize interaction among cultural strata, an argument that only serves to underscore the fact of difference. The struggle to gain recognition for lower-class and even middle-class culture—or at least to make the dominant classes less smug in their cultural possessions—has yet to be, perhaps can never be, concluded. And class distinction in culture as well as society continues on, despite all onslaughts, for these serve mainly to mobilize culture warriors in both the populist and elitist camps, not to confront our history past and present.

* * *

With all its venerable antecedents and adroit metamorphoses, populism is not the most vigorous ideology of culture at work in our time. Multiculturalism must be granted that status, despite or because of its under-theorization and rhetorical excess, for its vagueness and hyperbole do it grateful service in a nation still grappling with the "American dilemma," race. Like all ideologies, multiculturalism feeds on the will to maintain or alter a state of affairs rather than the will to describe it accurately.[13] There are differences, to be sure, between yesterday's cultural pluralism and today's multiculturalism, but each expresses a desire for ethnic survival by glorified and protected distinctiveness. In addition to its most egregious weakness, the assumptions it shares with racism about indelible group characteristics,[14] it is indistinguishable from ethnic boosterism, encouraging unabashed self-vaunting as a means of uplifting marginal groups. The downtrodden were long encouraged by social reformers to claim political and economic equality with dominant groups; they are now emboldened by pluralist ideologues to preen themselves on cultural "difference."

One might prefer to speak of America more neutrally as a "polyculture," on the model of William McNeill's term, "polyethnicity."[15] The term is to be preferred to "multicultural" if it helps dispel the notion that America's diversity represents a special case. The concept of polyculture addresses the normal processes of cultural diffusion, not only between societies but within them. In world-historical perspective, plural ethnicities have been the norm for all major urbanized societies, except perhaps Japan: "Only in remote and barbarous lands did ethnic homogeneity prevail." Plurality was the accepted situation until the eighteenth century when, for complicated demographic reasons, according to McNeill, "the nationalist idea of claiming rightful sovereignty for 'the people,' i.e., for those who shared a common ethnic heritage" became the model not only for Europe but eventually for its colonies in their quest for liberation. In the postcolonial world, renewed nationalism has come to be seen as a growing threat, but it may merely be a form of regretful resistance to the more general trend toward greater polyethnicity, not only in European nations forced to import alien cultures along with their "guest workers" but in America, land of constitutive immigration. The real issue, as McNeill pithily frames it, is whether polyethnic societies can depart from another long-standing norm, the socioeconomic hierarchy of ethnic groups: "Equality and freedom to be different are difficult to reconcile, especially when traditional cultural characteristics and patterns of education fit ethnic groups for some jobs and disqualify them for others.... So far, efforts to sustain equality in face of actual differences in skill and custom have met with very limited success."

In the absence of political and social equality, claims for cultural recognition are put forward as a substitute gratification, yet more substan-
tive gratifications have been available. Social scientists have recorded the
travails of numerous plural societies in which one group tyrannizes the
other(s), but these are matched by others, such as Canada and Brazil, in
which cultural interaction and blending take place even under conditions
of domination or hostility. America has been favored as well as beset by
its history as a nation of continual immigration, where even the later Ice
Age influxes from Siberia would have encountered, blended with, or
displaced earlier ones. Although historians such as Oscar Handlin have
detailed the psychic and other costs of immigration, and others such as
John Higham have recalled the harshness of the confrontations, the pattern of contact, conflict, and eventual interdependence persists.

Polyculture is to America what its creed of tolerance and inclusiveness
is to its politics—often subverted but too deeply rooted to be long sup-
pressed. The colonial period already showed American variousness in
its regional cultures, English, Dutch, French, and Spanish, nor were they
long kept apart by distance or competition. A synthetic imagination
showed itself early on: the Spanish padres converting the Southwest
were quick to incorporate indigenous building techniques and local cults
into church design and ritual; later, the Georgian culture of the colonies
was modified by the Jeffersons and Monroes, who treasured their French
furnishings, books, and ideas. The mixed West African traditions among
slave and former slave communities interfused with the popular culture
of minstrel shows and bordello entertainment to generate an indigenous
American art, blues and jazz. Culture circulates throughout society in
the most promiscuous manner, to the consternation of pluralist assertions
of ethnic distinctness. One has only to consult wide-ranging surveys such
as Ann Douglas's *Terrible Honesty: Mongrel Manhattan in the 1920s* (New
York, 1995) to sense the vitality—cutting across class and racial lines,
while ultimately leaving them in place—of this "mongrel" cultural impulse. The borrowings and blendings among contributory ethnic
streams, like those between the folk and fine arts, are particularly enriched in America by the sheer numerosity and relative freedom of minority groups. We were and remain together and apart, culturally
interactive while remaining socioeconomically separated.

The strongest force for cultural disparateness in this as in other industrialized nations is not ethnic multiplicity but class stratification. People go to shows, choose reading matter, and buy decorative objects they
can afford and that speak to their ideas of what is appropriate to their
standing, and these in turn are produced by artisans and industries with
their tastes and resources in mind. Although this understanding remains
the tacit and governing force in daily operations in the publishing, home
furnishings, and entertainment industries, culture talk seems to require

repeated reminders of it.[16] Racial and ethnic as well as class markets receive due attention from the culture industry, but these offerings are consistently found wanting by ethnic spokesmen, who proclaim their own images of group identity.[17] Often joining them in producing querulous critiques of media and other public images of minority cultures, multiculturalists extend the long tradition of interethnic contention without contributing generously to the equally vigorous forces of cultural exchange and partial fusion. This motley development, which advances with or without the blessings of ethnic ideologues, has been called by Higham "pluralistic integration," and although this paradoxical concept may not satisfy multicultural theoreticians, it describes a process that is happening all around us.[18]

* * *

Multiculturalism has proclaimed diversity for its own sake a virtue in culture as well as society, but the assertion or vision of cultural unity remains perdurable. What is perhaps unexpected is that this position, long associated with conservative patriotism and reactionary nativism, is matched in the ostensibly more democratic populist mentality. Michael Lind is the most recent in a line of populists to put forward the view that America has a "common national culture," the development of a successful assimilation process that, he predicts, will be extended as a "racial melting pot."[19] His account of the shared popular culture lies somewhere between the harmonics of Whitman's "America singing . . . varied carols" and the sterner strictures of the "cultural literacy" movement in the educational sphere. Addressing a widely perceived shortfall in educational outcomes, E.D. Hirsch, Jr., and his foundation have promoted "cultural literacy" as required knowledge of founding truths about the American experience, part of the basic data necessary for shared communication. Current reports of the actual state of affairs—as reduced to the absurd in comedian Jay Leno's interviews with young people who don't know how many moons the earth has, much less who wrote the Declaration of Independence—suggest that these facts will have to be far better disseminated before they can constitute a common culture.

The contents of Lind's American folkways, moreover, do not inspire confidence that they would be fully accepted even if better promoted. Many Americans, including myself, do not avail themselves of most of these resources without thereby constituting a marginalized group. Lind's list includes American manners, "the plain, just-folks style"; "American cuisine, [which] reflects heavy Southern and Southwestern influences"; national holidays (which, however, have lost much of their aura through official calendar manipulation, so as to become mere occasions for long weekends); sports (although these regularly replace each other as our "national pastime"); "common knowledge[,] what 'every American knows' " (more accurately, what every American doesn't know); and above all the American language ("one of the dialects of North American English," along with white, black, Hispanic, and Asian-American variants, so that ethnic-English speakers are presumed to switch to and from the "American" dialect at will). Most of these lie open not so much to the rebuke of partiality as to that of triviality: election campaigns and voting, military service, shared memories of the Great Depression or successive wars, while not universally engaged in, are closer to the core that holds a nation together.

Lind's perceived, or recommended, constituents of a common culture are, moreover, marked by class associations that the populist seems determined to ignore. Sharper than the aroma of a national cuisine is the pungent sense of class distinctions in American cooking—one need only compare the homey food sections of most newspapers with the chic recipes and restaurant reviews in *The New York Times* and other upscale publications (not to speak of Martha Stewart's elegant prescriptions for rising elements of the middle class). More significant, one need only apply for a white-collar job speaking nonwhite English to gather that some North American dialects are more American than others. Far from enjoying a common base that underlies its social variants, American popular culture (Lind's focus) is riven by middle-class strivings for differentiation from the lower classes, so that, in a negation of this negation, youthful rebellion against parental values leads suburban kids to rap music fandom. Meanwhile the upper classes carefully maintain lifestyle distinctions—nowhere so evident as in stadium skyboxes and "class"-segregated transportation—while cultural discourse heartily flaunts the common touch.

Further doubts about the soundness of his chosen culture arise from Lind's animus against the fine arts. In an article independent of his book (*New York Times Book Review*, March 14, 1999), he exults in the demise of "the Romantic and modernist religion of art, and the marginalization of its central figure," the artist as prophet or hero. Although there is something to be said for personal demystification—although not for resentful relishing of the artist's coming extinction—the scorn extends to high culture itself: "To be sure, cities are still building monumental art museums and subsidizing symphony orchestras—but they also throw away tax dollars on convention centers that frequently are just as empty as the culture palaces." The author here stands as the tribune for long-standing populist resentment, the rage of the little man despoiled by politicians, big business, and arty elitists who skim his hard-earned wages and ignore his own cultural claims. (His target, current promotion of the arts and their public endowments, will be considered in the next chapter.)

We need something more generous in spirit than visions of a common culture expressing impulses not much higher than class resentment.

* * *

If, as I have maintained, America's is a polyculture, an inorganic array of many contributory parts, with points or moments of fruitful fusion; if it is resistant to normalization according to any one segment, even that segment that purports to speak for the whole community; if it is class divided as well as ethnically and racially complex, then we need a concept of culture that acknowledges not only its ethnic variety but its social utility, while retaining a sense of the stability and, in evolving forms, permanence of the system as a whole.

The strongest recent reinforcement of the idea that cultural differences are inherent in class societies and useful in satisfying social needs has been made by the doyen (until his recent death) of French sociologists, Pierre Bourdieu. Although his major work, *Distinction*, has gained currency for its extensively researched demonstration of the workings of class, Bourdieu does not join his more radical followers in employing the social facts thus unearthed merely to demystify upper-class and highbrow snobbism (although he engages in such flurries, too). He sets out to report survey results confirming the existence of

three zones of taste which roughly correspond to educational levels and social classes: (1) *Legitimate* taste, i.e., the taste for legitimate works, here represented by *The Well-Tempered Clavier* [etc.], which increases with educational level and is highest in those fractions of the dominant class that are richest in educational capital. (2) *"Middle-brow"* taste, which brings together the minor works of the major arts, in this case *Rhapsody in Blue* . . . and the major works of the minor arts, . . . more common in the middle classes (*classes moyennes)* than in the working classes (*classes populaires)* or in the "intellectual" fractions of the dominant class. (3) Finally, *"popular"* taste, represented here by the choice of works of so-called "light" music or classical music devalued by popularization, . . . is most frequent among the working classes and varies in inverse ratio to educational capital (which explains why it is slightly more common among industrial and commercial employers or even senior executives than among primary teachers and cultural intermediaries).[20]

The terms employed here will seem both familiar and strange, but we cannot cite the evident differences between American and French classes and indicative artworks to evade the implications of this research. Two qualifications suggest that applying the principle that different classes have different tastes requires considerable flexibility: the one, that educators and other members of the intelligentsia—Bourdieu calls them the "dominated fractions" of the "dominant class" (p. 92 and elsewhere)—

are linked by educational attainments ("educational capital") to upper-class taste; the other, that upper- and middle-class businesspeople share in popular culture by virtue of their limited or specialized education.

I leave it to social scientists to weigh the massive survey data *Distinction* deploys to support its simultaneously commonsensical and ironically barbed thesis. As for the overtones of elitism ("legitimate works, minor works") that may alarm the more egalitarian reader, Bourdieu's ambivalence about distinction has eluded many an enthusiastic supporter: "Any legitimate work tends in fact to impose the norms of its own perception and tacitly defines as the only legitimate mode of perception the one which brings into play a certain disposition and a certain competence. Recognizing this fact does not mean constituting a particular mode of perception as an essence" (p. 28). Though neither esthetic disposition nor esthetic value is an "essence," that is, a category that escapes historical formation, there are, nevertheless, "legitimate" artworks, not merely in the "socially constructed" sense (legitimated by convention) but in their operation—works that impose challenging requirements for their perception, based on the learned competence of the perceiver. As in de Saussure's linguistics (to which Bourdieu alludes in the above passage), art like language is conventional and ultimately arbitrary, but there are differing degrees of competence in its usage.[21]

Bourdieu's sociological esthetics acknowledges not only arbitrary distinctions but profound differences that his more radical following finds hard to accept.[22] Recognizing that works of a certain kind require a high degree of cultural competence should lead one with Bourdieu not to undercut their merit but to deplore "the unequal class distribution of the capacity for inspired encounters with works of art and high culture in general." In his equally influential concept of education as class-stratified "reproduction," in which "all **pedagogic action** . . . *is, objectively, symbolic violence insofar as it is the imposition of a cultural arbitrary by an arbitrary power,*"[23] the little word "all" makes "symbolic violence" both a red flag for progressive educators and, in broad anthropological perspective, a necessary element in human socialization. Although education—whether socializing the young or sophisticating the elite (and potentially others)—involves "arbitrary power," it is essential to any concept of civilization, while also lying open to greater democratization.

Both the snobbish, domineering use of cultural taste and its functional role in group maintenance are inescapable in a class-ordered society. Moreover, the skewering of class distinction is not to be selectively applied, for all classes employ their tastes as simultaneous markers of identity and exclusion—lowbrow versus highbrow, and middlebrow versus both. Paramount in Bourdieu's approach is to regard social differences as always already present, with various forms of culture fulfilling (among other functions) a legitimating or reconciling role for each group.

Culture doesn't create class divisions, nor can it heal them, but it supplies the means for living out different social trajectories.

The existence of these "zones of taste" and their class mapping becomes visible on inspecting the arts in America today, as they would at any time in the past. Recognizing them for their social functions would help clarify a number of recent developments that have been obscured in the so-called "high/low" debate, where class associations have been strangely avoided, no doubt in an effort to transcend them. Discussion has largely been framed in art history terms, starting with the history of modernism. Here the penetration of elite art and literature by popular images and diction has been taken as an exemplary first stage in the blurring of such distinctions. For a politicized version of modernist experimentalism, the distinction between elite and popular is itself ideologically oppressive, so that artists may, indeed should, ignore received canons of high or low taste. So influential is this egalitarianism in art production, criticism, and display that contemporary art, even selected impressionist and modern art, has gained a considerable following, to judge from attendance figures at a number of recent exhibitions. (The heady claim of certain curators that it has become a mass phenomenon does not require detailed correction.) In this democratic campaign, little has been said about changes in the audience for such experiences, changes that have to do with rising educational levels, incomes, and social identities. In the absence of such considerations, the debate has become as idealist—removed from material realities and their behavioral consequences—as that which Marxists have deplored in traditional esthetic discourse. I shall try to make such connections without falling into the Marxist traps of causally linking art and economics, or into the vaguer culture-as-reflection theory. Bourdieu's formulations make it possible to register elements of the social world surrounding cultural behavior that would seem inescapable, were they not systematically avoided in the prevailing cultural discourse.

* * *

The class distribution of American culture does not replace the vigorous activity of ethnic, racial, and other specialized audiences, but the changing fortunes of these groups in the course of their assimilation leads to class reorderings that have cultural consequences. Ethnic cultural institutions have, of course, long existed: Jewish readers, for example, have had and, in reduced numbers, still enjoy their newspapers, magazines, and publishing houses. Some of these acquired the wider reach of *Commentary* and Schocken Books, as Jewish intellectuals gained national prominence. At a further stage, when Jews became increasingly assimilated into the middle and upper-middle class and into what may be called the European-American ethnicity (see below), cultural items with subtle ethnic markers, such as the films of Woody Allen or *The Graduate*, become popular by softening Jewish traits or anxieties so as to seem typical of these classes. (In earlier popularizations of Jewish experience, such as *The Jazz Singer* and *Abbie's Irish Rose*, Jewish themes remained explicit problems in search of solutions.) Other ethnicities follow this pattern as they become secure in the middle class: witness the popularity and to some degree idealization of potentially demeaning portrayals of Mafia families by Italian-American writers and filmmakers (at first a cause of anxiety among older members of this ethnicity, and still a source of chagrin for some of its activists). Even the proverbial poverty and alcoholism of Irish-Americans are, after the handsome social rise of this ethnicity, esthetically redeemed in the stylish best-sellers of Frank McCourt. What authorizes the wide public expression and mainstream acceptance of ethnic experience is the establishment of a solid base of middle-class respectability by the ethnicity in question.

This process extends to racial minorities, in keeping with the expansion of the middle class to include African- and Asian-Americans and other formerly excluded groups. Works of black literature have proliferated, and heightened attention has been accorded to a substantial though recherché body of work from antebellum America to the flowering present. But black literature didn't become prominent in the national culture because of the attention accorded to the underclass, nor even at the urging of its academic and political advocates, but in tandem with the growth of a black middle class. Black authors such as Ralph Ellison and Richard Wright were appreciated for a time by a mass audience but didn't achieve the bestsellerdom of a Toni Morrison or Alice Walker, at a time when the middle class, augmented by blacks, became receptive to another of its constituent voices—until, it might be said, such writers had themselves become middle class. The emergence of minority work on a national scale regularly derives from developments in social position, so that the call for recognition raised by the proponents of "diversity" may make sense primarily as a program to accelerate a social process well under way by its own momentum.

Increasing recognition of a wide range of minority achievements is consistent with the emergence of a new majority grouping in the country, partially displacing the dominant WASP ethnicity while retaining a complex ethnic base. Ethnic communities of European origin, once deemed "unmeltable" by hopeful pluralists, are, according to social researchers such as Richard D. Alba, demonstrating the continued viability of assimilation by high rates of intermarriage among themselves (that is, from one ethnicity to the other within this cluster) and by the resulting consistency in their political, social, and cultural behavior. Many of these

"European-Americans" (on the model of African-, Asian-, and Latin-Americans) have enhanced their assimilation by rising in class, so that different attitudes and behavior are observable between their lower- and middle-class segments. On the middle-class level, the highly touted revival of ethnic values can be seen as a demonstration of what Alba follows the sociologist Herbert Gans in calling "symbolic ethnicity": "it is difficult to see the cultural expresssions of identity as more than a fragile and thin layer alloyed to a larger body of common American culture, with its complex class and place variants."[24]

The downplaying of religious and ethnic differences within this emergent ethnicity has been accompanied by firm resistance to special treatment of minority groups that have had greater difficulty following the archetypal Americanization pattern. Yet this, the largest ethnicity and one that constitutes the bulk of the middle-class market, has opened itself to infusions of minority culture, as screened through the culture-industry filters that disseminate *The Color Purple* and *The Joy Luck Club* in print and visual media. Despite their suspicion of the more strident forms of ethnic culture, like gangsta rap music, the European-Americans generally profess respectable opinions on racial and other ethnic claims to equality.[25] With all its openness to diversity, however, the middle-class segment of this ethnicity seems inclined to maintain established mainstream tastes, as carefully regulated as its residential and schooling patterns. It is thereby implicated in the culture war that has recently stirred so much animosity, perhaps exceeding its true weight.

The presence of both social broad-mindedness and impatience with cultural extremism among this group may have more to do with its own division along class lines than with simple continuation of traditional interethnic friction. As James Davison Hunter has characterized the struggle between cultural conservatives (the "orthodox") and progressives, "the progressive alliances tend to draw popular support from among the highly educated, professionally committed, *upper* middle classes, while the orthodox alliances tend to draw from the *lower* middle and working classes."[26] In esthetic tastes and moral attitudes, European-Americans have been split along class lines, with the upper echelons, encouraged by their highly educated offspring, more tolerant while the lower, with continuing economic anxieties, remain entrenched in censorious positions. Although culture war discourse only dimly reflects the very different class standing of progressive and orthodox cultural warriors, class distinction within an ethnic context offers a stronger explanation of the culture wars than ethnic tensions or political and religious positions by themselves.

* * *

Class stratification, overriding racial, ethnic, and regional diversity, has always complicated America's cultural texture, but an intensification of the class factor was introduced to the cultural scene by socioeconomic developments peculiar to late capitalism. As numerous statistical studies have reported, inequality in wealth has become greater in the United States, even while the nation enjoys unexampled growth, relatively low unemployment, and widespread prosperity. Although the consequences of socioeconomic polarization for the lower classes have been the focus of concern, another aspect of the technologically induced transformation calls for attention. Certain readings of the data suggest that at least as much of the evacuation from the middle class has occurred in an upward as in a downward direction. Since midcentury, the gross numbers and relative proportions of the upper-middle and upper classes (variously defined: see chapter 3) have markedly increased, with the elevation of highly educated professionals into the former and even the latter categories.

This grouping (to be further characterized below) includes people with disposable income sufficient to become not only experiencers but owners of fine or at least expensive art, with comparable investments in commissioned architecture, interior design, et cetera. In accordance with the scale of their investments, they are not merely passive but often vigorously active cultural consumers, joining in if not leading the prevailing cultural discourse. When a segment of the bourgeoisie, very different from their forebears in educational background, enters the market for high-end goods and performances, total demand for cultural goods of the legitimate type grows. With the emergence of new stalls in the marketplace, a new cadre of art-makers comes into existence, so that the number of Americans characterizing themselves as artists now numbers in the millions (1,671,000 in the 1990 census). The idea of artists as *producers*, replacing the disused term "creators," is born. The late-twentieth-century boom in cultural production arose to serve the needs of an expanded affluent population, with an enlarged layer of ultrarich patrons at the top and an even more enlarged stratum of professionals— often themselves cultural workers and educators—making up an exciting market for cultural goods.

How have culture producers and their dissemination regime—which I shall, in the next chapter, follow Bourdieu in characterizing as the "field of cultural production"—framed their response to these new class realities? The strongest ideological theme in American culture talk—amounting, in the view of historian Michael Kammen, to a consensus if not an orthodoxy[27]—is that categories such as high-middle-low no longer apply to cultural experience. Going beyond the truism that tastes in a diverse cultural scene become more readily mingled, and beyond the lazy assumption that cultural mixing corresponds to a blurring of class lines in

America, this purported description aspires to prescriptive force. Under-writing esthetic with political imperatives, a taboolike negative has been elevated into a positive critical norm. The proscription of esthetic hier-archy in creation and criticism becomes the warrant for cultural produc-tion that deliberately, gaily mingles whatever comes to hand. With no criteria for selection, the best taste at this time is that which scorns "good taste."

One doesn't have to go far to find deeper sources of this esthetic ide-ology. As new styles develop to satisfy, justify, or otherwise reward a rising social class, considerable anxiety attaches to the status claims of both producers and consumers. To ease the transition to acceptability, a tacit agreement has been reached to disclaim explicit esthetic standards for judging individual artists or their works, or the styles and media in which they function. The situation is similar to that recorded by Alan Wolfe's and other surveys of middle-class tolerance in judging others in the social sphere: with all the table thumping of the "moral majority," the prevailing attitude toward most behaviors is "live and let live." Rob-ert Hughes has described the postmodern idea of the art object, whose "basic cultural assumption [is] that a work of art can exist for any length of time, in any material (from a stuffed goat to a live human body) anywhere (on a stage, in front of a TV camera, underwater, on the sur-face of the moon, or in a sealed envelope), for any purpose (turn-on, contemplation, amusement, invocation, threat) and any destination it chooses, from the museum to the trashcan."[28] American polyculture reaches full expression in this protean idea of the artwork, accessible to all comers in the newly emergent upper classes.

Yet as any observer of the art scene will testify, an openness to variety and a disclaimer of esthetic norms by no means diminishes the necessity of judgment or the intensity of controversy. A recent *New York Times* sampling of professional opinion was headed "Is It Art? Is It Good? And Who Says So?" (Oct. 12, 1997). Unanimity was reached on a Republican congressman's assertion that "Art is whatever people want to perceive it to be," although few in the culture industry will follow him in the corollary that "that doesn't mean that the Federal Government should fund it." When, however, the responses of the artists, academics, and critics interviewed are grouped according to their professional roles, the continued operation of strong esthetic requirements becomes vivid.

The artists were vigorous for subjective or expressive criteria: "It's art when . . . doing it makes me feel good" (Richard Prince); "We see art as fun. As long as it gives us some kick, it goes" (Alexander Melamid); "its role [is] therapy for the artist" (Louise Bourgeois). Academic art histo-rians were united in affirming the authority of their profession, employ-ing the conventionalist, "interpretive community" approach to esthetic value or scholarly truth (a claim of authority based on expertise): "It is art if it is called art, written about in an art magazine, exhibited in a museum or bought by a private collector" (Thomas McEvilley); "there has to be consensus about good art among informed people" (Robert Rosenblum); "There's a consensus as to what art is in most periods, but it's not made by the man in the street. It is formed by those deeply concerned with the substance of art" (William Rubin). Among the practicing art critics, a restrained assertion of criteria derived from content—the makings of an objectivist account—were in evidence: "certain questions come into play—what it's about, what does it mean, why was it made. . . . If you can get good answers to those questions, it's art" (Arthur Danto); "If it's not visual and it's not viceral and it's not communicative, it's not a work of art" (Karl Katz); "something is a work of art if it is made with the declared intention to be a work of art. . . . That does not determine whether it is esthetically rich or stupidly banal" (Robert Hughes). The artistic activity of self-expression, the learned attribution of canonical standing, and the daily clamor of rival reputations are as robust as ever, but are conducted under a principled agnosticism regarding objective value.

Esthetic agnosticism, the distinctive feature of cultural discourse in contemporary America, in its careful avoidance of class taste along with other divisive designations, may seem to reflect a growing classlessness in the nation. Yet the refusal of esthetic norms and categories, motivated by populist hostility to cultural snobbery and to the classes that practice it, is as imbued with social judgmentalism as are its targets. As in other cultural spheres, esthetic tolerance, without extinguishing underlying loyalties and oppositions, accords well with the emergence of new claimants to cultural standing who are not yet secure enough socially or educationally (with respect to art) to insist on a particular style or canon as the hallmark of their ascendancy. So their trumpeters in the cultural world proclaim a principled inclusiveness toward high and low art that itself becomes the marker for inclusion and approbation within the favored grouping.

Another evasion of class taste, while seeming to acknowledge and then reject it, is based, in varying degrees of explicitness, on the false inference from studies such as Bourdieu's that since esthetic norms are always historically conditioned—"socially constructed," in current academic jargon—they are ultimately merely arbitrary.[29] There's no denying that high culture can be and has been used as an instrument for bolstering the social standing of dominant classes. Yet Bourdieu's and other investigators' evidence indicates that people of all classes think and act distinctively along class lines and make cultural choices accordingly, so that some measure of utility or benefit must implicitly be promised or actually derived from the distribution. How do relativistic or populist culture critics deal with evidence that class distinctions in culture are both systematic (in relation to each other) and regular (in their persistence, with determinate changes, over time) while maintaining that they are purely arbitrary and class biased?

It is the tendency of current cultural discourse both to disdain class distinctions in taste and to reinstitute them in critical practice. Esthetic agnosticism is extended beyond refusing judgmental norms for artists and artworks to a more sweeping embrace of all cultures, irrespective of class or other group designations. Yet the celebratory tone of many an art establishment account of recent American creative work, particularly in the visual arts—for example, the well-worn mantra that the center of modern art shifted in the postwar period from Paris to New York—indicates a judgment that this high-cultural phenomenon is a very good thing indeed. This accession to eminence has been acclaimed in terms suggesting a national achievement, as in the title and format of the Whitney Museum's exhibitions of twentieth-century arts under the rubric *the American Century*, yet the reasons for pride in this collective accomplishment would have to be staunchly argued to a goodly portion of the general public. Far more evident than the national marks on this putative predominance of contemporary American art is its class marking. Produced for, bought and sold in, and displayed within an upscale market for luxury goods, this art is stamped with the taste markers of a class culture. But even the more socially conscious among the art journals and museum curators have difficulty moving beyond broad esthetic approval of this style or set of styles to the recognition that its class designation involves them in approbation of a class culture. Even when a radical art journal such as *October* pillories the commercial aspects of the cultural scene, it makes no reflection on its premise that contemporary American art is a worthy enterprise, to be, on the whole, favorably judged.

Much the same pattern of simultaneous esthetic agnosticism and class-cultural judgment is visible when lower-class culture is at issue. An academic cottage industry called "cultural studies" has arisen to celebrate the creative responses of working-class people to their inundation by what is variously termed "mass culture," the "culture industry," or the "capitalist hegemony." Modifying the standard intellectual disdain of mass culture—especially the erstwhile leftist critique of the culture industry as fostering an ideological hegemony over the workers' minds and hearts—new left critics have discovered in it potential resources of social change, doubtless to compensate for the failure of other forms of revolution. The academic subfield now officially designated Cultural Studies, in the wake of the French theoretician Michel de Certeau,[30] has called attention to working-class creative modifications of the culture industry's banal products, as in karaoke-like adaptations of commercial pop music and tinkering with standardized design in the housing projects. This "semiotic guerrilla warfare" is said to express working-class vitality in resistance to manipulation by mass media, but it seems more derivative than creative. It is inevitably a response to or modification of products and productions introduced by other, stronger culture-making enterprises. The Cultural Studies vaunting of lower-class culture—at best a discovery of a saving grace in an otherwise deplored condition—is accompanied by a willed indifference to the parasitic element in its innovations.

Current cultural discourse is thus marked by vigorous but masked promotional efforts on behalf of the culture of the upper classes and by cautiously defensive gambits on behalf of lower-class culture. Its esthetic agnosticism easily admits class judgments while refusing any suggestion that one class's culture could be by any standard superior to another's. Yet what do these affirmations of upper- and of lower-class cultures amount to but an implicit (and at times explicit) devaluation of middle-class culture? Continuing the long tradition of intellectual disdain of "masscult," present-day culture critics hardly waste breath on the mainstream movies, literary potboilers, and other staples of middle-class experience.[31] The prevalence of cultural hierarchy is still the operative assumption in this discourse, neatly disguised by protestations of openness to diversity and by visceral shrugs at the idea of disciplined esthetic judgment.

Amid this unsettled state of mind, hostile toward yet expressive of class cultures and their relative standing, the latest entrant group in the cultural field has received only scattered attention. This is a class that has the financial and educational resources to manipulate and be manipulated by the widest range of cultural images and experiences. The emergence of all that is roughly lumped together as postmodernism did not fall from the sky as a revelation but responds to the emergence of a new class in the social systems of advanced industrial nations. The Chippendale skyscraper and the Marilyn Monroe silk screens weren't designed to show appreciation of either classic taste in design or mass taste in film idols. They were rather incorporations (in more than one sense of the word) of varied class tastes into a new style that gratifies a new class. They call up not the symbolic richness of middle- and lower-class life, but rather the "how quaint!" response of recognition and amusement by a knowing group. It is the culture of this new class that remains to be credited and examined if the contours of contemporary American culture are to be fully represented.

* * *

These misdirections by those who seek to overcome cultural hierarchy, yet settle into long-standing positions in a class-oriented cultural field, would be less lamentable than other intellectuals' efforts in behalf of the masses were it not for an area of neglect that calls for concern. A sociologically inclined critic of pop music, Simon Frith, has called attention to the unseemly consequences of abstention from value judgments in the arts, both high and low.[32] In divesting themselves of the presumed oppression of esthetic norms that seem to denigrate low culture by the standards of high, critics both within and beyond the realm of pop music have neglected the need to distinguish good and bad in popular and other cultures. Following up on Bourdieu's association of advanced education with the experience and judgment of high culture, Frith points out that education and experience within popular culture circuits produces *fans*. These "people who have invested time and money in the accumulation of knowledge" become formidable judges of good and bad in their favored sphere. Although they need no encouragement in pronouncing value judgments, these judgments might be put on firmer ground with the guidance of intellectuals in determining esthetic value.

If there's a shortfall in intellectual discourse on popular culture, then, it lies in failing to participate in and guide the judgments that people of all classes are continually making in their cultural experience. This lapse from the intellectual vocation—which involves being of service to the classes with which distinct types of intellectuals, traditional and organic (to use Antonio Gramsci's much cited terms) are connected—is noticeable not only with respect to lower-class but also to middle-class culture. As Edward Shils puts it, with delectable irony, "Quite the opposite of what is believed by those who see mass culture . . . as an infection doing harm to the culture of the educated class, it is the poor culture of the educated classes which is doing harm to mass culture."[33]

It is self-evident that critics of popular culture, like those in other cultural registers, make critical judgments all the time, that the elaborate system of awards and best-seller lists lends force to these judgments, and that esthetic competition is the lifeblood of this as of other industries. Yet the question of quality in the popular arts has been avoided on much the same grounds that have made "quality" a nonce term in discussion of the fine arts. It is apparently elitist to aim at raising or even maintaining standards in either realm. Hence, to cite another example, the detached acceptance by cinema historians, though not by all journalist reviewers, of the film industry's descent into brutal culture (Shils's term seems the only appropriate one here), leaving a broad critique to moralistic partisans such as Michael Medved. The bad effects of esthetic denial on low culture—but with implications for high—are baldly put by Frith: "the more celebratory the populist study [of popular culture], the more patronizing its tone, an effect, I think, of the explicit populist determination to deny (or reverse) the usual high/low cultural hierarchy. . . . [W]hat needs challenging is not the notion of the superior, but the claim that it is the exclusive property of the 'high.' "

Frith's own efforts to compensate for this shortfall may not be fully convincing, but they are a step toward an esthetics of popular culture that may encourage revived esthetic attention in its traditional sphere. There are, indeed, estheticians such as the philosopher Richard Shusterman working in both realms.[34] But efforts to take popular culture seriously by reducing the two realms to one (Shusterman) or by employing the same evaluative principles (Frith) ignore the differing social functions of these cultures. It is not merely the art objects or their socially generated auras that are different but the social needs they serve: different classes, consisting of very different people, require different things from their cultures, and specific objects and events in each realm must be evaluated as they serve those needs. The all-American formula, "different strokes for different folks," holds in the cultural realm as strongly as in any other: populist veneration of the common man notwithstanding, historically conditioned groups enjoy vastly different things. The question that esthetic agnosticism too easily abandons is: How well does each culture, or its individual elements, serve its class audience?

My purpose, given a limited competence in fine art as well as in pop, is not to answer this question but to challenge the assumptions that have made for its avoidance. The proposition that all value judgments are illegitimate has become widely avowed because it seems to offer relief from intellectual aloofness to the cultural choices, especially in pop music and Hollywood films, to which the intelligentsia itself has become increasingly inclined. In this, it has been slow to recognize its own recent social transformation. From being an outsider grouping, the American intelligentsia has not only gained status in an information society but has become organically connected to a new and rising social group, which I shall follow others in calling the New Class. Since many of these educated and educating people are not totally weaned from the low or middling culture of their classes of origin, they hold up their own mongrel taste as the model of cultural value generally: we like everything from Monteverdi to U2 and beyond, and see no reason to give any of it up. The esthetics of blurring (to adapt Kammen's term) is germane to the practices of a class highly endowed both financially and educationally, and trained to tolerance in the cultural as in the social sphere by an intelligentsia that speaks from it and for it, since it is largely a part of it.

NOTES

1. Michael Kammen, "Culture and the State in America," in Gigi Bradford, et al., *The Politics of Culture* (New York and Washington, 2000), p. 119. Kammen elsewhere performs yeoman service in setting out museums' powerful political and symbolic functions: *Mystic Chords of Memory: The Transformation of Tradition in American Culture* (New York, 1991).

2. Lawrence H. Fuchs, *The American Kaleidoscope: Race, Ethnicity, and the Civic Culture* (London and Hanover, N.H., 1990), p. 276.

3. Dwight Macdonald, *Against the American Grain* (New York, 1962), p. 3.

4. Edward Shils, *The Intellectuals and the Powers and Other Essays* (Chicago and London, 1972), p. 232 ff. Although the first of these tags subtly conveys value judgment by means of a pun, an inspection of professional wrestling or current action fims would find the second term loaded but accurate.

5. A singular exception to these evasive categories is the approach in Herbert Gans's *Popular Culture and High Culture: An Analysis and Evaluation of Taste* (New York, 1974), which gets beyond the diad in its title by listing high, upper-middle, lower-middle, low, and quasi-folk cultures, adding "youth culture" for good measure. Although this sociologist's descriptions of these cultures are at best impressionistic, his explicitness about the correlation of class and taste remains exceptional in American sociology.

6. Paul J. DiMaggio, "Cultural Entrepreneurship in Nineteenth-Century Boston," in Paul J. DiMaggio, ed., *Nonprofit Enterprise in the Arts: Studies in Mission and Constraint* (New York and Oxford, 1986), pp. 41–61; Lawrence W. Levine, *Highbrow/Lowbrow: The Emergence of Cultural Hierarchy in America* (Cambridge, Mass., and London, 1988).

7. See Robert Hughes, *American Visions: The Epic History of Art in America* (New York, 1999), p. 99 ff.

8. Steven Conn, *Museums and American Intellectual Life 1876–1926* (Chicago and London, 1998), p. 29; Conn's account of the motives of the founders of New York's Metropolitan Museum does, however, bear out DiMaggio's strictures.

9. Michael Kazin, *The Populist Persuasion: An American History* (New York, 1995), p. 6.

10. The oppositional impulses in folk and popular culture are grist for the mill of the Cultural Studies movement; for a more dispassionate account of the populist politics of vernacular music, see Ron Eyerman and Andrew Jamison, *Music and Social Movements: Mobilizing Tradition in the Twentieth Century* (Cambridge, 1998).

11. Larzer Ziff, *Literary Democracy: The Declaration of Cultural Independence in America* (New York, 1981), p. 98.

12. Leo Marx, *The Pilot and the Passenger: Essays on Literature, Technology and Culture in the United States* (New York and Oxford, 1988), pp. 262 and 287.

13. This distinction, highly suspect in postmodernist theory, may be supported by comparing Horace Kallen's formulations of cultural pluralism (multiculturalism's predecessor) early and late: the antiassimilation polemic of his writings leading up to *Culture and Democracy in the United States* (New York, 1924) contrasts sharply with his mellow approach to the philosophical problems of unity and identity, *Cultural Pluralism and the American Idea* (Philadelphia, 1956).

14. Walter Benn Michaels, *Our America: Nativism, Modernism, and Pluralism* (Durham, N.C., and London, 1995) is like a bath of cold water, if not acid, on this point. A more nuanced account of the course of pluralist thinking is John Higham, *Send These to Me: Immigrants in Urban America* (Baltimore and London, 1984 [1975]), ch. 9. Higham's rebuke of multiculturalism, not only for its departure from America's foundational universalism but for its willful ignorance of class divisions, is bound together with predictable responses from black, Latino,

and feminist historians in "Multiculturalism and Universalism: A History and a Critique," *American Quarterly* 45 (1993), 195–256.

15. William McNeill, *Polyethnicity and National Unity in World History* (Toronto, 1986); the quotations that follow are from pp. 15, 34, 76 and 82.

16. For a salutary recent reminder, see Thomas Strychacz, *Modernism, Mass Culture, and Professionalism* (Cambridge, 1993), p. 53 ff.

17. A representative selection of these criticisms—for example, of Hollywood portrayals of Italian-American life in Mafia movies—is Ishmael Reed, ed., *Multi-America: Essays on Cultural Wars and Cultural Peace* (New York, 1997), whose governing spirit might be summed up thus: no cultural justice, no cultural peace. In this spirit, one section is devoted to essays on "Friction: Inter-ethnic, Inter-necine, Fratricidal,"—a bracing reminder of long-standing processes still at work.

18. Higham, *Send These to Me*, p. 242 ff. I have tried to focus this account of multiculturalism on its degree of applicability to American cultural experience; for the political and social dimensions of this movement and its baleful conse-quences, see John J. Miller, *The Unmaking of Americans: How Multiculturalism Has Undermined the Assimilation Ethic* (New York, 1998).

19. Michael Lind, *The Next American Nation: The New Nationalism and the Fourth American Revolution* (New York, 1995), p. 298; quotations that follow are from p. 265 ff.

20. Pierre Bourdieu, *Distinction: A Social Critique of the Judgement of Taste*, trans. Richard Nice (Cambridge, Mass., 1984 [1979]), p. 16; citations that follow are made parenthetically.

21. For Bourdieu's elaborated esthetic theory, see *The Rules of Art: Genesis and Structure of the Literary Field*, trans. Susan Emanuel (Stanford, Calif., 1995 [1992]), in which sociological reduction of esthetic norms to elements of a conventional system is accompanied by painstaking formalist analysis of works by Flaubert and others for their organic unity of form and content.

22. Bourdieu's linkage of both educational and economic capital to legitimate taste has led some left-leaning commentators to reject the class-culture correlation altogether: see John Frow, *Cultural Studies and Cultural Value* (Oxford, 1995), p. 40 ff.

23. Bourdieu and Jean-Claude Passeron, *Reproduction in Education, Society and Culture*, trans. Richard Nice (London and Beverly Hills, Calif., 1977 [1970]), p. 5; boldface and italics in the original.

24. Richard D. Alba, *Ethnic Identity: The Transformation of White America* (New Haven, Conn., and London, 1990), p. 121.

25. See Alan Wolfe, *One Nation After All: What Americans Really Think . . .* (New York, 1998).

26. James Davison Hunter, *Culture Wars: The Struggle to Define America* (New York, 1991), p. 63.

27. Michael Kammen, *American Culture/American Tastes: Social Change and the 20th Century* (New York, 1999), p. 100.

28. Robert Hughes, *The Shock of the New* (New York, 1991 [1980]), p. 334.

29. The most vigorous statement of this esthetic position, notable for the sharp political stance that emerges from its deconstruction of esthetics' political bur-dens, is Barbara Herrnstein Smith's *Contingencies of Value: Alternative Perspectives for Critical Theory* (Cambridge, Mass., 1988); for the defense of her norm-laden

antinormativity, see *Belief and Resistance: Dynamics of Contemporary Intellectual Controversy* (Cambridge, Mass., 1997).

30. Michel de Certeau, *The Practice of Everyday Life*, trans. Steven Rendell (Berkeley, Calif., and London, 1984) is the canonical text; the writings of Stuart Hall, John Fiske, and others in this line are collected in numerous readers for popular college courses.

31. It is true that another small academic cottage industry devotes itself to learned commentaries on such phenomena as soap operas, folk-rock lyrics, and the like, but these redemptive efforts display only interpretive ingenuity, not a change in wider intellectual attitudes.

32. Simon Frith, *Performing Rites: On the Value of Popular Music* (Cambridge, Mass., 1996); quotations that follow are from pp. 9 and 16.

33. Edward Shils, *The Intellectuals and the Powers* (Chicago and London, 1972), p. 121. Shils's formulation of the role of intellectuals in society follows the classic position of Max Weber that they are necessary to and thus necessarily implicated in any social order. On the adversary tradition of modern intellectuals, much has been written, not only in celebration but in derision; Joseph Schumpeter's *Capitalism, Socialism and Democracy* (New York, 1942), ch. 13 is definitive in the latter vein. On the two traditions in American cultural history, the final chapter of Richard Hofstadter's *Anti-intellectualism in American Life* (New York, 1963) makes a sweeping summation.

34. Richard Shusterman, *Pragmatist Aesthetics: Living Beauty, Rethinking Art* (Lanham, Md., 2000 [1992]). Frith discusses Shusterman's esthetic elevation of the practical values of low culture and links it to Bourdieu's account of fine art's functional value for the upper classes (pp. 17–18).

2

The Field of Cultural Discourse

"I delight in general in artists, but I delight still more in their defenders."

—a character in James's *The Tragic Muse*

Culture talk goes on all the time but it isn't always the same talk. The ancient impulses toward tradition and change, realism and abstraction, edification for all or for the worthy, are argued in the here and now as they have always been, but an updated lingo makes them harder to recognize. Eternal themes may seem alien to everyday participants in the field, whose daily life is filled with news—reputations up and down, new publications and anticipated performances, et cetera—whose patterns have settled into workaday regularity. Between these poles of the perdurable and the quotidian, gradual substitutions in words, ideas, and personnel occur, whose compounded effect is discovered only well along in the transition. The new paradigm functions not to bring all comers into line, as with cultural policies decreed in tyrannized nations, but as a set of opposed assumptions, norms, or behavioral choices, within which considerable freedom is permitted but whose parameters define the limits of the possible. This structured system of culture talk I shall call the field of cultural discourse, linking it to other appropriate descriptions of culture in technologically advanced societies.

The most familiar of these discourse phrases often use the term "world," with a comfortable assumption that it constitutes all that counts. Thus we speak of art world, literary world, and so on without considering how close to being literal the metaphor may come. The current elaboration of human and material elements in these subfields makes the word seem appropriate. Irving Sandler's chapter on "The Art World in the First Half of the 1980s" adds to the art historian's formal description of stylistic trends and major figures a painstaking enumeration of the human and material entities surrounding the artist and his work.[1] These include collectors, institutional and individual, galleries and dealers, auction houses and their specialists—the market, in a word. Beyond it lies a more ramified dissemination system, consisting of museums and their curators, university departments and their scholars, journals with their editors and critics, foundations and their panels for awarding grants—all those engaged in determining esthetic value (although the concept is all but disused), which the market converts into monetary terms. It is this support system, intermediary between producers and consumers, that conducts and regulates cultural discourse in the art world; talk goes on with gusto among artists and among consumers, of course, but it is shaped by the prevailing currents of discussion in the intermediary network. Much the same structure operates, with modifications appropriate to their materials, in the literary, theater, music, and other "worlds."

Though such a system seems normal and natural, it is worth recalling that there is nothing inevitable or traditional about this state of affairs. It is true that by the start of the nineteenth century, William Blake was already (in the prologue to his epic *Milton*) inveighing against "Hirelings in the Camp, the Court & the University," who determine artistic values "by the prices they pretend to give to contemptible works, or the expensive advertizing boasts that they make of such works." Yet throughout the history of the arts, artists have been important contributors to the culture talk of the day—often, from Vasari to Roger Fry and from Ben Jonson to T.S. Eliot, with decisive force in setting artistic directions. A distinguishing mark of contemporary cultural discourse is the weakening of creative people's participation in the structured discourse, whatever they may be saying in their working and leisure mutterings. A glance at any of the anthologies of twentieth-century commentary on modern art shows them dominated by artists' writings on their programs and ideals. It would be difficult to assemble a similar compendium for the art theories of the last third of the century.[2] In the literary world, John Barth's 1967 declaration of a "literature of exhaustion" opened a trail of discussion (much of it, including the author's own subsequent statements, devoted to speculation on what he had meant), but rarely thereafter do novelists and poets compete with the torrent of academic literary theory. A period of vigorous intellectualizing—"theater of the absurd," "theater of cruelty," et cetera—by theater folk in the sixties and seventies was followed by almost total withdrawal from large conceptions on their part. There have, of course, been assertions enough of intent and aspiration on specific productions, yet artists' current participation in the culture talk of the age—as distinct from their engagement in political controversy at critical moments—is mainly at an informal rather than programmatic level.

In part this change in participation has been willed by the artists themselves, in keeping with the assertive naïveté of much art-making in our time. Their withdrawal into silence comes partly in response to the oversophistication of theoretical language in academic and even journalistic writing on art and literature.[3] Minimalist and conceptual artists and writers do, indeed, strive to justify their radical reduction of expressive means, but their written documents are designed to substitute for artworks withheld or reduced to banality. Most practitioners display an understandable tendency to mind their own business and just paint or write, and this devotion to doing rather than explaining has been encouraged by a pattern of exclusion, more or less deliberate, practiced in another part of the field, the institutional.

A case in point: of about 265 participants (an approximation, because some of them appeared multiple times) in recent forums on the public role of culture sponsored by the National Endowment for the Arts, reported in the volume *American Canvas*, only fourteen were artists.[4] Because the NEA's precarious political situation, which brought this project into being, called for marshaling support among civic and business leaders and strengthening links to foundations and arts institutions, it is not surprising that representatives of these entities abounded. But the paucity of artist participation in discussions of the state of our culture, mounted by the official upholder of the nation's arts, is testimony to their status in the serious business of cultural policy making, marketing, and dissemination. The gathering of institutional representatives of this magnitude conveys the message that culture is too important a matter to be left to individuals, let alone mere artists. And this not because institutional spokesmen bear a philistine scorn of artists—their pronouncements suggest the opposite—but because the scale of cultural operations in the public sphere dwarfs individuals, even when they are as numerous as the current population of artists and consumers.

The significance of this changed composition of the participants in today's cultural discourse will emerge, I trust, in what follows. It should not, however, be inferred that a relative absence of the artists' contribution necessarily leads to intellectual deprivation. Many a challenging idea and significant disagreement circulates within the support system that presides over cultural discourse, enough to provide a lively intellectual context for creative work as well as for marketing and dissemination. To assess the relation between these ideas and the system that circulates them, it is well to apply to the French sociologist Pierre Bourdieu, who followed up his account of class tastes in *Distinction* with a series of studies of the production and promotion of art itself. In *The Field of Cultural Production*, Bourdieu offers a way of looking at cultural discourse in which even its less intelligible formulas become part of a meaningful whole.[5] Taking up the long history of controversy among artistic schools and critical camps, mainly in nineteenth- and early twentieth-century France, Bourdieu shows the remarkable symmetry of the positions taken, each matched by its opposite and apparently generating it (although he is cautious in providing causal explanations). His contribution to this well-known history is to grasp a pattern in the messy world of creators and critics, marketers and collectors: a structured social system with an internal logic that explains both the excessive vehemence and the subsequent irrelevance of the famous controversies in art history.

In a structural view, the cultural field of a society at any given time is organized in a fashion, on the whole unplanned, as a working order with its own dynamics of self-adjustment and self-maintenance. An artist or critic entering the field looks about at the range of activities and ideas and takes a position within it, either aligning himself with an existing one or attempting to formulate a distinctive one. In this welter of markedly individual assertions, each position depends on the others and would have little content if detached from the contentious community in which it is enacted. Bourdieu joins a series of philosophers such as Ludwig Wittgenstein and literary scholars such as Stanley Fish who have established the interpretive community, whether within scholarly disciplines or communication in general, as the locus of meaning for individual speech acts.

Yet this "space of position takings" (a term developed on p. 131 ff.) is no purely formal arrangement, designed merely to keep the ball rolling, as it were, and maintain the participants in a spirited and to some degree rewarding activity. It also corresponds, in ways that are palpable to view yet difficult to causally trace, to the range of activities actually under way in the production and distribution sectors. The divergent methods of "large-scale and restricted production" (p. 115)—Bourdieu's terms for cultural work destined for the public or for the connoisseurs—may be seen to lie at the heart of many a critical distinction. In the nineteenth century, it generated contention between bourgeois and art-for-art's-sake positions, in the early twentieth, between officially sanctioned and avantgarde norms. The basic opposition between "orthodox and heterodox" work is modified in each period, but until recently it served as the organizing matrix in debates over traditional canons and striking innovations in style and taste. And the shifting positions on experimental and "consecrated" work may be traced through the support system of critics, academics and other authorities (p. 123 and passim).

Bourdieu's categories provide a foundation for the curious pattern discerned in modern art by numerous art historians. Peter Bürger, prominent among them, describes the twists and turns of the modernist avant-garde and the pronouncements that justified them. In scrutinizing the "tradition of the new," as it has been called, Bürger points to a contradiction in its characteristic activities. Avant-garde artists' basic strategy is, of course, shock—both as an assertion of independence and as a gesture of opposition to the powers that be—whether defined by class or politics. Yet all shocks are temporary; repeated shocks are absorbed and become dulled by familiarity. In sum, as Bürger puts it, "the shock is 'consumed.' "[6] Hence the need for new styles, new moves in the game, to arouse attention, to provoke, and ultimately to sell. "Ultimately" can be a heartbreaking word, to be sure, but the time lapse between the upstart's challenge to orthodox taste and the collector's acquisition of once outrageous work has been diminishing through this period, until the production and marketing of scandal has been routinized. The sharpest impression to be gained from such recent events as the Brooklyn Museum's *Sensations* show of cutting-edge British artists was the ritualized performance of all involved (well expressed by the show's title, one sense of which suggests causing a "sensation"): the exhibitors (museum officials more than the artists themselves), the public officials (in the mayor's outraged tones and threats of defunding), and the arts community (supporting the principle of free expression but wary of being dragged into a provoked conflict). All seemed to be acting out previously scripted texts, hence the suspicion that they were playing roles in a structure that alone constituted their actions' meaning. A more cynical interpretation would hold that the meaning of these performances, in pragmatic terms, was the uptick in museum attendance and the gain in market prices generated by all the publicity.

Hence the remarkable end-of-an-era change in the historical structure Bourdieu and Bürger have well described: the traditional opposition between orthodox and heterodox art has been abolished in favor of a functional symbiosis between them. Deliberately provocative works, such as cross sections of animal carcasses or mutilations of the exhibited artist, are now systematically produced and consumed, often in production facilities that ape large-scale enterprises. (Andy Warhol provided an honest label for his studio, the "Factory.") Literature and music are still composed in private spaces and under esoteric principles, but the concept of art for art's sake, which generated past tensions between supporters of orthodox and heterodox art, has largely disappeared. Although the degree to which modern art has become popular is still a matter of conjecture, it is observable that avant-garde art has become commercial art— observable by no sign so strongly as that the terms themselves, "avant-garde" and "commercial," have become nugatory in culture talk. In the marketplace, only the distinction between what Bourdieu calls the "consecrated" as opposed to the "youthful" avant-gardes continues to function, expressed in the resentful talk of the latter group. But even here, the inflated pricing for abstract expressionists and major pop artists stimulates a general inflation in the market, in which even the more recent entrants can share.

Yet the historical structure of large-scale/restricted, orthodox/heterodox positions in the cultural field continues to operate, with modifications instilled by forces at work in society at large. A new duality has been instituted, although it has yet to attain the rich vocabulary of stylistic distinctions and ideological abuse developed in the long campaigns of modern art. The opposed concepts may be called *community art* and *personal art*, although terms to express them have yet to become formulaic. Foundations such as the NEA have interpreted their responsibility to serve the largest number of citizens possible by supporting ethnic and regional artists and performance groups considered not merely individually outstanding but representative of entire communities. In so doing, they respond to the aspirations of minority groups to gain recognition for communal achievements, whose creators are celebrated insofar as they advance those aspirations. Judgments of this kind range from historical surveys of jazz and blues as expressions of the black community to women artist groups' body counts of the numbers of their sisterhood displayed at various venues, in which statistical representation counts more than other attributes.[7]

In promulgating the value of art as the expression and possession of communities, a negative view of personal art emerges to flesh out the structured opposition. Direct attacks on the dignity and aura of the artist such as the populist Michael Lind's (see chapter 1) are rare, but a more profound undermining of the artist's authority as the controlling source of his creation—since Roland Barthes's and Michel Foucault's announcements of the "death of the artist"—have become standard in American literary scholarship. Aligned with these conceptual trends is the shift in the favored tools of art-making from the painterly brush to the variety of electronic and construction media now favored by artists themselves: when video art and land art require technical crews as well as industrial resources, the visual arts follow cinema in the direction of collective rather than individual expression. Nor have these developments been lacking in theoretical foundations. The most widely quoted and perhaps generally favored view of art at the turn of the millennium is probably Walter Benjamin's essay, "The Work of Art in the Age of Mechanical Reproduction"[8] on the desirability of arts that exploit the capacities of technological reproducibility. A new battery of expressive means enabled film, video, and photography to run painting, if only for a time, off the map. (Recent reports indicate that a return to painting has, predictably in a field's dynamics, become one of the latest trends.) It also allowed the aura surrounding artworks, and to some degree the authority of the artist, to become as fragile as that of creative work in the film industry. Although the aura surrounding the paintings of a Mark Rothko or Andy Warhol remains high, the factorylike conditions of the latter's work join with other trends to make personal creativity all but an irrelevance. Indeed, the temporarily influential films of Warhol were executed by Paul Morrissey, but few cared to acknowledge him as their creator. Even in the poetry section of the literary field, the popularity of live performances by demotic enthusiasts has made racial and ethnic coloration into as important an element of poetic merit as more traditional features of the craft.

The relationship between community art and personal art bears the marks of a calculated opposition within a structured field, but they also display tendencies toward fusion, especially as one of them becomes the more powerful force. Thomas Frank's *The Conquest of Cool*[9] describes the program developed in the advertising and media industries to deal with the sixties' explosion of resistance to mass marketing, by exalting individualism in every kind of behavior, including consumerism. The business approach was simple: capture the enthusiasm for personal style and attach it to mass-produced, mass-media offerings. Thus cars and other products with production runs in the millions were marketed as opportunities for self-expression and personal freedom. Just as with the apparent conflict and easy reconciliation of these impulses toward collective behavior and self-determination, the interactions of community art and personal art constitute a theoretical dichotomy but allow a pragmatic unity. The call by playwright August Wilson for a greater allotment of roles for black actors and for other reapportionments makes a neat superimposition of individual ambitions and collective claims. Women artists produce images of women—often using their own faces and bodies—to reveal and resist their shaping by dominant social forces, simultaneously filling personal and collective roles. These painted but more often photographic images are accompanied and sometimes replaced by printed slogans of personal wit taking the form of gnomic collective wisdom (to make a charitable construction of their frequent banality). The MacArthur Foundation fellowships, once colloquially referred to as "genius" grants, are now almost exclusively devoted to people representing institutions with projects for socially approved goals: individual genius is now defined by engagement with a community.

Given the division of labor in the arts establishment, it was to be expected that the twin directions in artistic practice would be expressed in culture talk—institutional personnel devoted to the community art vocabulary while artists remain steeped in the language of personal art. But a curious pattern of redistribution operates in this discourse, much the way that individualistic and vaguely bohemian language was co-opted by corporate sponsors of mass-produced goods. Since so much of their working life and after-work socializing is focused on institutional sponsors and the grants process, a proportionate measure of artists' social and private communication employs community shibboleths. With the premium placed on art that speaks of or for group experience—in the performance arts and literature as in visual media—how could creative people fail to adopt the institutional discourse, especially when in many cases their own inclination that way lies? Meanwhile, institutional manifestos are sure to rehearse the mantras of individual expression as watchwords of their high mission.

If any broad impulse characterizes turn-of-the-millennium American culture—akin to what formalist estheticians have called the "dominant" of a period style—it is this infusion of personal art with the values and rhetoric of community art. It is entirely appropriate that the culture of a hugely successful democratic society, particularly one as polyethnic and otherwise segmented as the United States, should be oriented toward the needs and tastes of the many groupings within it. When the normal practice of governmental as well as private foundations aiming toward the greatest good for the greatest number is to add one group after another to its client list, the promotion of community art seems inevitable and right. More subtly and humanely than in tyrannical regimes, artists are called upon to serve and speak for the people (or favored kinds of people) and, given the liberal idealism of some and the financial encouragement for others, they have ample reason to comply. In the future, the culture of our time will be covered in art histories as one in the long succession of major periods, after Medieval and Renaissance, Romantic and Modern. We can only speculate on how well its artworks will show up in this implied contrast. But if every age has its art, an art expressing its social as well as esthetic values, this phase of American culture will surely be distinguished for developing and justifying expressive means to proclaim group identities.

* * *

These vistas are undoubtedly shadowy, though not for that reason unworthy of contemplation. Assessment of our cultural discourse is more solidly placed when reviewing the vexed recent history of the National Endowment for the Arts to see how it has changed to accommodate community art.[10] To recall what every schoolboy knows, in order to point out some curious anomalies: right-wing attackers and mainstream defenders of the NEA have displayed stronger affinities than they might wish to avow. Beyond focusing on the politically useful obscenity issues of the Robert Mapplethorpe and Andres Serrano photographic provocations, conservatives targeted the standards and operation of the NEA's selection process. They invoked democratic principle to protest that it favored an art providing satisfactions not for the taxpaying public but for a select segment of society, and that it was staffed by an unrepresentative body of experts. (The word "class" was never mentioned, but the word "elite" quite a bit.) In defense, the NEA and the cultural establishment spoke of the endowment's past and present services to society, the rarity of its departures from social acceptability, and its commitment to the values of its patrons, the public. Both sides agreed, then, on the norms of "large-scale" rather than "restricted" cultural production, to apply Bourdieu's terms, and of "heteronomous" (for the public) art rather than "autonomous" (art for art's sake). The expressive freedom of the individual artist was asserted by all, in varying degrees of fervor, but the role of these artists in representing their respective groups was an unavoidable subtext, either in derogration or defense. Mapplethorpe's depiction of the gay community's ethos in practice was explicitly attacked and defended; Serrano's status as a Latino artist was a background consideration in judging his anti-Christian imagery.

Although critics of the endowment grudgingly granted the free-speech norm, they reserved the right to be selective in its application, based on communal standards of acceptable behavior. To this, certain defenders, particularly the more vocal artists and institutional heads such as the public theater impresario Joseph Papp, asserted more stridently than has long been heard in the land the absolutes of personal art—the liberty of the artist to follow and articulate his vision.[11] And Papp showed the courage of his convictions by renouncing the NEA's support when it seemed to cave in to political pressure. There were, after all, distinctions to be discerned between the almost uniformly communal discourse of the political spokesmen, liberal and conservative, and the personalist mottos of some artist participants in the debate.

Peculiarly absent from this paean to expressive freedom, however, was an affirmation of esthetic value: that what the artist at his best expresses is the good, the true, and the beautiful; that what Mapplethorpe and Serrano contributed could be described in such terms; that an artwork supported by public funds might succeed or fail to justify the outlay on its merits as a work of art. The closest approximation to such a claim was made by an expert witness in the Cincinnati obscenity trial that extended the controversy; under prosecutorial prodding, she employed formal design categories to confirm the esthetic status of a Mapplethorpe photo of a urination ritual. The formalist terms raised courtroom laughter, given the bodily functions portrayed, but at least they attempted to establish that art is not identical to, and can be judged on other grounds than, its subject matter, and that ethical considerations operate apart from and may sometimes make way for esthetic ones. Such ideas have rarely been employed to justify the NEA's disbursements, though they always purport to be given for artistic merit, for the defenders have joined the attackers in subordinating esthetic norms to pragmatic, group-associated ones.

* * *

In the absence of agreed-upon (or even argued) esthetic standards, many a superlative has been employed to justify the endowment's record of supporting worthy creative people, as determined by the panels of experts judging its grants. But this argument falls flat, not because the experts are themselves under a cloud in the conservative campaign to discredit an elitist capture of public funds, but because judgments of the artist are not esthetic but reputational. (Only works can be considered beautiful, though certain people are said to produce such works regularly.) To claim that a grant honors the artist, not a particular work—after which he is entirely free to express himself—only fuels the populist charge of a coterie catering to a coterie. So the NEA has embarked on a long and partially successful campaign to show how the public benefits from the arts and its support of them. Community art norms here are baldly pragmatic: employment generated by cultural institutions and their associated commercial activities; urban revitalization furthered by arts center projects and resulting downtown pedestrian life; redistribution of nationally collected taxes to underserved areas of the country; et cetera. Who can quarrel with such tangible and worthy effects from purportedly ethereal and even frivolous things such as artworks? Financial benefits to the community from arts support, enthusiastically hyped, have, however, been skeptically treated in close economic studies.[12] But with such arguments, the NEA has been able to stave off political extinction and maintain its budget at about half its heyday rate.

Yet this depleted state—coupled with a decline, even in a booming economy, of private arts support—has little pleased the cultural establishment, although artists have become sadly resigned to it.[13] Thus the elaborate public forums of 1995–96 that issued in the *American Canvas* report. Here the institutional representatives were encouraged, or encouraged each other, to look inward, to criticize their own failures to supply the public's needs—whether by regional, ethnic, or other demographic criteria—and thus, worst of all, their failure to build public support for the arts so as to advance claims on the public purse. Now it was not right-wing populists who mouthed the dreaded word "elitist," but many in the arts establishment itself.

The tenor of self-criticism was, upon closer inspection, not as antielitist as reported in the *New York Times* (Oct. 13, 1997: "Study Links Drop in Support to Elitist Attitude in the Arts"); for journalistic purposes, it was a "cultural activist" in the Latino community whose rhetoric made for pungent citation. The prevailing lament was for the lost opportunities to make contact with and gain support from other institutions in the public and private sectors—hence the inclusion in these forums of business and local political figures who stand as models of the desired relationship. At no point was failure connected to the quality of the artworks the NEA has subvented, as though the degree of public appreciation of the foundation's efforts were quite independent of its success in providing esthetically satisfying works. Thus in this discourse, standards of community art—comprehensive and proportional representation and distribution—replace the esthetic norms of personal art. In the marketplace, whether for low culture or high, works of art that many people approve gain lofty sales figures or high admission prices, but in the nonprofit art sector, the equivalent of prices—tax dollars—are spent without considering either public approval of or the esthetic quality of the works produced with their support. Though the very notion of esthetic quality now sounds archaic, it once served as the explicit rationale for the NEA's foundation: the endowment would encourage esthetically valuable work that would otherwise be neglected in the open market. Lacking either the inclination or the grounds to argue that the work it supports is esthetically valuable, the NEA's defenders expose not only the weakness of their political position but also the structure of current cultural discourse.

The absorption of personal art by community art is not confined to socially dedicated institutions but is more widely found in the art field, among critics, scholars, and artists themselves. Because they do not operate according to esthetic norms, either for high culture or low, foundations must rely on professional peer panels to ground their selections. But since these in turn operate without expressed or agreed-upon esthetic norms, the inherent value of approved work is less apparent or arguable than its representative status in a communal context. Like all grantors, the NEA aims for "excellence" and does the best it can to select and support artists who have gained or may gain a reputation, but it can make no reasoned judgment of the esthetic quality of the work they produce, any more than it may take into account its thematic content. (The latter proscription is, to be sure, regularly breached on behalf of work on approved themes, though it has become a sensitive area in the wake of the politicized scandals.) Nor does it take a measure of the public appreciation of its subvented works, beyond attendance figures. (Of this, more in a moment.) Its proponents' call for greater connection to the public is, then, a pep talk for stronger public relations efforts, not for a provision of good or better art. In the former area it is at home, for this is the realm of community art talk; in the matter of esthetic quality, the personal art sphere, it has nothing to say.

A recognition of such anomalies and absences has prompted at least one foundation in the cultural establishment to seek enlightenment. The Pew Charitable Trusts' project for studying the arts in America with a view, among other things, to understand the "impact of arts on individuals" (*New York Times*, Aug. 2, 1999) suggests that at least some in the field are aware of how little it knows about personal art. To be sure, its concept of what might be significant in this area is crude and akin to pragmatic norms: it seeks "the stories of how one person's life is changed" by art. Yet it may be on the right track: "Some of the scholarly work the Pew intends to sponsor would try to establish the long-held but unproven belief in the arts world that cultural programs are valuable intrinsically and not simply as leisure activities, as many Americans see them, or as economic engines, a more recent view." One has only to read this bald account to sense how far our cultural discourse has come from long-standing ideas of art.

We may wish this institution and its researchers well in their effort to discover at last art's intrinsic value—a starting point might be Proust's meditations on the subject in *Remembrance of Things Past*—yet it is unlikely, given the broader context of esthetic judgment in contemporary America, that it will find its way. In the absence of esthetic consensus, and in a direction away from its mandate to support unpopular as well as popular art, the NEA has increasingly applied demographic criteria to target or justify its programs. Following other, though not all, non-profit foundations' imperative to serve all segments of the public, it thereby becomes committed to attendance figures as measures of success. What does the record show about these tactical efforts and their underlying assumptions about the arts?

The NEA's own summaries suggest that the nation's arts activity, much of it attributable to foundation support, has vastly increased, but without a measurable corresponding appreciation by its consumers. Citing James Heilbrun and Charles M. Gray's study, *The Economics of Art and Culture*, the NEA reports that consumer spending on the performing arts almost doubled between 1975 and 1990, but by 1991 was experiencing a decline (5 percent in that year). The decline in symphony concert attendance began earlier, dropping in 1989 and thereafter more than 10 percent from a peak in 1986.[14] Although public response, perhaps wearied by excessive ministrations, shows signs of weakening, the proliferation of cultural venues showed, for a time, little discouragement. Although government, foundation, and personal giving for the arts has had its ups and downs, the report's generalization about its encouragement of creative activity shows becoming modesty: "increases in the number of artists and arts organizations over the past three decades has far outpaced the growth in both public and private support." Indeed, the desire of artists and arts entrepreneurs to present their best efforts

to the public has been fervent: the number of professional dance companies, for example, rose from 37 to 400 from 1965 to 1994 (with a similar
proliferation of opera and theater companies and orchestras). Yet their
aspirations have not always been fulfilled by success in attendance and
subvention: in the dance field, for example, "the number of ballet companies declined from 331 in 1986 to 281 in 1992." As with the figures for
symphony concert attendance, these data imply that institutional support
for the arts has fostered admirable growth in cultural production but
rather less in consumption.

In this market as in others the audience has satisfied its own needs
and interests, selectively supporting arts and artists according to its
tastes. To these tastes, class-bound in the view maintained here, the NEA
and the arts establishment generally pay scant attention, devoting themselves to the tastes and interests of specific groupings, such as ethnicities,
women (or feminist constructions of this amorphous group), and geographical regions or urban areas. Yet the discriminations in class reception of the arts go on, impervious to the communal rubrics maintained
for ideological purposes. To see how they operate, consider the fortunes
of the urban arts centers that have proliferated in the past decades (more
precisely, since the midsixties, in emulation of New York's Lincoln Center).

These impressive testaments to urban revitalization range from the
$187 million New Jersey Performing Arts Center to the Myrna Loy Cen-
ter in Helena, Montana, housed in a renovated former county jail. It
would be heartless to belittle the public-spiritedness of these efforts or
the inherent value of the artistic experiences they foster. But recent accounts of their operations offer a bracing portrayal of class esthetics in
action: "The Louisville Orchestra, which has been struggling, has had to
seek other performance spaces when the center wanted to make room
for touring Broadway shows"; "last season, the Florida Orchestra could
obtain only three of its desired twenty-one dates in the Tampa Bay Performing Arts Center because of touring shows"; the Bass Performance
Hall in Fort Worth, not waiting for ticket sales to determine how to
allocate space and time for classical music and other recondite fare, in
its inaugural season "offers Milton Berle, Judy Collins, the Flying Kara-
mazov Brothers and the ballet 'Romeo and Juliet' danced on ice" (*New
York Times*, Dec. 6, 1998). The gains in civic participation and in multi-
plied "leisure activities" from these imposing ventures are undoubted
goods, but it is hard to resist the impression that local arts institutions
have been left no worse or better off than they were. What does emerge
from these well-calculated moves to satisfy the interests of the middle
class is that arts center managers are perfectly attuned to the class tastes
that culture talk and the arts establishment rigorously avoid.

If "the arrival in the 1960s of a huge generation of artists, technicians, and administrators, [was] driven not by funding or economic gain, but rather by their own desire to produce art" (to quote an economist cited in *American Canvas*); if the proliferation of artists and performing arts groups has not consistently provided works that meet the tastes of the general public (however vaguely defined); if building cultural centers merely reinforces existing patterns of leisure activity, if these hard facts obtain, we may well ask, whose needs and desires are being served by the arts establishment in America? In a sanguine view, it is all of these constituencies, named and ignored in cultural discourse: the upper clas- ses, which favor high culture (and are happy to have government sup- port for elite venues such as the Metropolitan Opera), the middle-class turnouts at the popular arts centers, the artist and arts institutional pop- ulation itself, of course, and the ethnic and other groups supported on ideological grounds. Enlarged cultural outpourings temporarily raise all boats, though selective attendance by audiences bound by class taste ultimately determines their failure or success. Although one may disdain the political motives and ethical rhetoric of the conservative assault on the NEA, it would be ostrichlike to disregard its expression of long nur- tured dissatisfaction by large segments of the citizenry with the minis- trations of the arts community on their behalf.

The closest the NEA comes to acknowledging the class distinctions in its operations is remarkable both for its recognition of and discomfort with the fact of class:

[T]he arts community has long labored under a stubbornly persistent class sys- tem of its own, one that continues to haunt the field: the recognition, palpable even in our democratic protestations to the contrary, that the audience for the non-profit arts remains highly skewed, betraying a demographic profile that tends to be older, wealthier, better educated, and whiter than a typical cross- section of the American public. (pp. 75–76)

Imagine another government agency summarizing its problems in a com- parable manner, confessing and lamenting the "class system" that directs a disproportionate amount of its expenditures for housing improvement toward the poor or of its small-business loans to the middle and upper- middle classes! Like other Americans, the arts establishment, as repre- sented by this report, is fully aware that high culture is a largely upper- and upper-middle-class pursuit, but it's not happy to acknowledge that support for the fine arts means feeding the already well fed. It did not take a Bourdieu to discover that cultural tastes are distributed along a socioeconomic scale, but it will take more than a new set of "democratic protestations" to bring self-confidence to an inherently class-driven en- terprise.

The NEA approach to the problem that "haunts" it is to make the arts more relevant to a broader segment of the population, especially non-white, less well-heeled audiences: "The challenge is to reach out to the majority of Americans who currently have no direct involvement with the professional, nonprofit arts, to expand the nation's cultural palette to include a full range of participatory activities, without losing sight of the standards of professional excellence that still have a role in providing benchmarks of achievement" (p. 163). This is to restate one of the founding and unimpeachable motives for government support of the arts: the cultural education of all, especially people who have had few opportunities to learn of and perhaps enjoy high culture. Its redistributionist rhetoric suggests the strategy by which this high goal is now to be pursued: since high cultural practices do not directly engage "the majority of Americans," that is, the lower and lower-middle classes, "a full range of participatory activities"—the arts and leisure activities they actually favor—are to be encouraged. Given the endowment's attentiveness to minority and regional groups, it is implied here that the challenge of cultural education is to be met by subventing popular arts such as jazz and folk crafts that are already established in ethnic taste. Here ideology and political lobbying work hand in hand: the arts establishment's liberal inclination toward advancing minorities and its hopes for political clout through enlarged attendance figures and community support are fully in accord with each other. But for all its pragmatic willingness to redress class imbalances by adding ethnic and regional fruits to its cornucopia, the establishment's strategy may be a flawed and even a naïve one.

With the shifting winds behind cultural spokesmen's power to influence national and state capitals, and with the open question of whether the newly favored classes, under any stimulation, might become vigorous in support of the arts, recent tepid responses to urban cultural centers, ethnic activities, and the NEA's public pronouncements suggest that its new strategy may be pursuing unreasonably high expectations. Moreover, the success of this strategy may prove an even less desirable outcome than the condition it was intended to correct. The campaign to shift endowment emphasis from "older, wealthier, better educated and whiter" people's culture to that of younger, poorer, less educated, and darker people may prove a Pyrrhic victory. It marks a decisive reorientation in the grand design of arts support over the larger part of the NEA's history: to "transmit the achievement and values of civilization ... and make widely available the greatest achievements of art," according to the congressional mandate quoted in *American Canvas* (p. 22). A government program created by an administration of the "best and the brightest," designed to distribute the values and achievements enjoyed by the upper classes to a wider portion of the citizenry, will have evolved into one that encourages other classes to maintain their diverse vernacular tastes.[15] The reality of class differences—flavored by ethnic diversity—will have been reinforced, in the absence of a clear grasp of the class structure of cultural taste.

* * *

I have commented at length on the National Endowment for the Arts' recent statements of purpose and tactics, not in the spirit of its detractors but in an attempt to see how they reveal more widespread current notions of culture in society. These elements of a discourse have yet to become universal in the nation's culture talk, nor even in the nonprofit, government, and foundation sector. But the NEA's recent accession to populist aims and rhetoric has strong parallels in the visual arts and literary fields, where defensiveness about "elitism" and popularizing slogans are current coin. In an era when pop music and mainstream films are taken seriously, not as social symptoms but as cultural forms on a par with any others, the voice of the people carries well in the land, magnified by critics, media, and politicians. In bringing together a cross section of arts professionals and public supporters (although not of artists, as noted earlier), *American Canvas* tells us much not only about the latest sallies in the culture wars but also about the state of cultural understanding in our time.

Is there a better way of thinking and talking about the arts? Assuming that a variety of cultural activities corresponds to the actual differentiation of social segments in a nation, it may be granted that the enormous diversity of the arts in America exists to serve, and in some measure succeeds in serving, those segments' desires and needs. Even before tackling the demanding task of determining how those constituents are best served—that is, on what basis the artistic offerings for their differing tastes are to be selected and evaluated—a prior step would have to be taken. The difficulty arises in determining, in an environment of ideological claims, what these social elements are: classes, ethnicities, regions, political constituencies, et cetera. The NEA, in line with other government agencies disbursing funds on a national scale, employs regional demographics, to which it adds, in reponse to the multicultural shibboleths of the moment, considerations of ethnic and racial distribution. It regards class segmentation as a problem that "continues to haunt the field," locating the "class system" not in the society it serves but in the arts establishment itself. What would a recognition that class in America is, just as it has been in every developed society, a fundamental fact of life propagate in culture talk and action?

Freed of its disused Marxist trappings in the wake of Bourdieu's studies, the class distribution of culture has come to be gingerly discussed, if not deeply studied, in cultural discourse. Talk in this vein has persisted through the past century, but has been dosed with ideological vitriol of several kinds. Modernist critics both on the right and left—ranging from T.S. Eliot and F.R. Leavis to the Frankfurt school and more orthodox Marxists—have derided mass culture for a host of sins, the main charge being that it is the product of a culture industry that decides for its own interests what the masses will enjoy, without allowing the latter to determine their own satisfactions.[16] More recently, post- or neo-Marxists such as Jean Baudrillard and Fredric Jameson still expose the alienating effects of mass culture, although, relabeling some of them as postmodernist, they are seduced by its power to convey the spiritual emptiness of the late-capitalist world. Another, more sanguine line of Marxisant thinking, the Cultural Studies movement, hopefully accords power to lower-class creativity in modifying industrialized products for the people's tastes and interests. Yet even among its more sympathetic critics, mass culture continues to be regarded as a problem rather than a legitimate provision for lower- and middle-class taste. Without adopting a Panglossian complacency, we may come to accept that, in light of its persistence and adaptability, mass culture is fairly effective in satisfying the publics it serves—in sum, that mass culture *is* lower- and middle-class culture, carefully modified for class, ethnic, and other subdivisions by designated providers in the culture industry. One need only compare television sitcoms such as *Frasier* or *Ally McBeal* with *The Drew Carey Show*, or any of the black sitcoms with their white counterparts, to see how efficiently targeted and exhaustively arrayed these provisions are, by class, race, and other social specifications.

In keeping with the vast scale and complex shape of the American middle class (a subject to be considered in the next chapter), its culture is almost as varied as America's itself, containing ethnic and regional varieties, adaptations of both folk and "elite" works (mixing elements of what Bourdieu calls "popular" and "legitimate" taste), and other testaments to the culture industry's demographic inclusiveness. In historical perspective, we might trace the process by which middle-class taste came to comprehend selected regions of the fine arts, as in its recent embrace of French impressionism, thereby escaping its traditional role as the object of avant-garde derision. Although it would be too much to claim, as some have done, that modern art has entered popular culture, versions of modern architecture, sculpture, and interior design have become familiar presences in middle-class homes and in public spaces serving primarily white-collar workers.

This broadening of middle-class taste has worked changes in the avant-garde, too, which over the last two centuries defined itself by opposition to the middle class, with an obligation to *épater le bourgeois* not only in art but in lifestyle and values. The initial post–World War II decades saw a heightened intellectual derision of these changes; among the most sweeping responses was Harold Rosenberg's alarmed declaration in the late fifties that "Kitsch has captured all the arts in the USA."[17] At this juncture, Dwight Macdonald's "masscult" and other pejoratives became standard. But the rise of pop and other easily accessible art movements, along with the revival of populist antisnobbism discussed in chapter 1 as the culture of blurring, effectively obscured the so-called "great divide" between high and popular culture. At present, there is a state of comfortable communion between artists and members of once hostile classes, who have even become prospects for their works: "The negative dialectic between avant-garde artist and audience . . . in its last, heroic efflorescence in the 1950s seems to belong to an ancient, almost forgotten period, whose attitudes are alien to us."[18]

To replace the long oppositional tradition of avant-garde and bourgeois esthetics, an apparently new discourse of high/low conflation has been instituted. A range of positions in the newly structured field has been duly taken up: there is no real difference between "legitimate" and "popular" art, merely arbitrarily imposed judgments; there is a difference but it's created by social inequality and furthers that injustice; there is frequent creative interaction between high and low arts, so that the distinction has been or can be broken down; there's room for all concerned at the great feast, so that snobbery must at all costs be avoided, et cetera—with intermediate positions filled in ad lib. A portion of the current discourse descends from the American populist tradition, as chapter 1 has recalled, and may be considered historically nostalgic rather than, as some prefer to think, cutting edge. Yet instability enters a discourse when consensus leaves the structure without a reliable antagonist: with elitism retired from the field, its opponents must scurry to distinguish their positions from each other.

A case in point is the array of views on modern art's relations with popular culture. Although it did not approach the intensity of debate over the Museum of Modern Art's 1984 exhibit of modernist primitivism,[19] discussion of the museum's 1990 *High and Low* show brought out many of the same oppositions. The exhibit and its accompanying volume[20] were at pains to display the variety of interactions between modern artists and popular culture, moving from cubism's incorporation of newspaper type and other commonplace materials to the variety of subsequent creative reframings. It also displayed the reverse moves, including the advertising industry's appropriations of modernist style and imagery. At home on this two-way street, the exhibit culminated with evidence for the debatable proposition that "American Pop art of the 1960s has become . . . genuinely popular" (p. 335). Although declining to avail itself of the abundant evidence of similar interactions in modern literature (Joyce, Eliot, et al.) and modern music (Bartok, Weill, et al.), the exhibit effectively undercut the proclamations of ideological critics that the long tyranny of modernist separation of elitist and popular art had suddenly been revolutionized by postmodernism.[21]

One cannot fault an enterprise as scholarly and sophisticated as the *High and Low* show, but its historical focus on the twentieth century limited its grasp of the history of cultural discourse. Although acknowledging in passing the Romantic roots of the popular culture question (p. 16), and devoting full coverage to nineteenth-century anticipations of popular themes in artistic caricature (p. 101 ff.), Varnedoe and Gopnik missed the opportunity to invoke a long and powerful strain in artistic theory and practice. As Charles Rosen and Henri Zerner make clear, "the mythology of nineteenth century art," positing the popular resources of artistic creation, was firmly established in the Romantic period. In its wake, high/low discourse persisted as a lively alternative to the more flamboyant avant-garde/bourgeois oppositions in creation and criticism.[22] All the high/low themes and images are there from the outset: folk art, historicist revivals, primitivism, exoticism (for example, Japanese popular art), the breakdown of genre hierarchy, the demotic challenge of photography—most of them have been on view for two centuries. For a historical exhibit on modernism to curtail a major strain in its heritage is almost as distorting as to proclaim the liberation of popular art and the people from the trammels of modernist elitism. The latter is merely a move in the field's discourse; the former avoids a perspective in which such ideological moves may be seen for what they are.

The reconciliation of classic adversaries such as the middle class and the avant-garde, the furtherance of deep and long symbiotic relations between high and low culture—these developments seem to offer a transcendence of class in a nation ever hopeful of a way beyond it. Yet in practical effects, class taste is still the norm, motivating the strategies not only of mass but of specialized culture producers. To counter these unwholesome social behaviors, the discourse of blurring fosters the birth of a new synthetic style, often calling it postmodernism, without recognizing that its advent at this historical moment may itself be a consequence of class. Although it would be premature to assign a strictly socioeconomic origin to postmodernism, its emergence in the decades that also saw the emergence of a new and vigorous class cannot be mere historical accident.[23]

The "rise of professional society" traced by historians over the last two centuries[24] has been extended in recent decades by the arrival of professionals exercising control functions in the advanced technology of an information economy. This grouping has been characterized in varied ways (to be summarized in subsequent chapters), but the presence of a new breed of well-educated and financially competent entrants to the upper-middle class quickly and untheoretically became manifest to potential providers of cultural goods. The expansion since the sixties of upscale publishing, especially in paperback versions of erstwhile academic books, the proliferation of LP and later CD classical recordings, even the temporary popularity of avant-garde European cinema (currently in recession) can hardly be accounted for otherwise. This broadening of upper-middle-class taste by the entry of a more discerning element had an effect not only on that class as a whole but on the artist community that had long kept a distance from it. The avant-garde welcomed the opportunity to supply rather than harry the bourgeoisie, and the strategies of pop art and its subsequent variants quickly proved effective. (The avant-garde's endemic oppositional tendencies received ample alternative channels for expression during the Vietnam protest period.) The class distribution of American culture was thereby maintained, but was modified in a way fully in accord with the emergence of a new class fraction.

After its long devotion to upper-middle-class culture (the "class system" it was eventually shocked to find itself in), the arts establishment became dimly aware of striking changes in that class itself. Though these institutions have some difficulty in discerning the precise contours of cultural classes, the needs of the educationally well-endowed professional and technological intelligentsia came to seem worthy of attention. It was hardly coincidental that programmatic support of high culture benefited not only the nation as a whole but especially the class that shows both broad interest in such arts and growing political clout to match its financial strength. This new class orientation was never made explicit and was instead identified as a strengthening of cultural provision for all—though its class distribution eventually became clear for all to see.

Culture talk in the institutional and other arts spheres rarely resembles the formulations offered here. Yet *American Canvas*'s demographics on its characteristic beneficiaries—"older, wealthier, better educated, and whiter"—leave no doubt that the arts establishment understands what every schoolboy knows about cultural distribution in America. Calculating the potential influence on public opinion along with the political strength of the social groups they serve, public and private foundations take account of class stratification when sufficiently alarmed. The current project of greater inclusiveness, couched as it is in the dominant rhetoric of multiculturalism, may seem to mark a retreat from attentiveness to the upper classes. Although minority groups and regional constituencies have become, for unimpeachable political motives, the new client groups, it is foreseeable that other classes are likely to be the actual beneficiaries of these efforts at cultural redistribution.

Of course, many an ethnic musical group and shoestring repertory theater will profit from a shift of resources from support of venerable opera and symphony companies to grassroots sites. But the greatest beneficiary of more varied and more widely disseminated cultural support is likely to be the New Class, as it spreads beyond silicon centers to the far reaches of the land. Its current generation of members stems from highly varied social origins, achieving upward mobility by their hallmark, educational capital. (The term, "educational capital," like "cultural capital of familiarity," "social capital of 'connections' " and other cognates of financial capital, introduced by Bourdieu in *Distinction* [for example, p. 360], has become something of a cliché; without commitment to their theoretical justification, I employ them as handy metaphors.) Their origins in the lower and middle classes, as well as in higher ones, produce a varied and apparently incoherent cultural taste: it's not unusual to hear them expressing preferences for both Mozart or Beethoven *and* the more esoteric pop music groups, or to find them at Shakespeare performances as well as poetry slams. Other peculiar features of their educational formation, including large doses of multicultural ideology acquired under current educational policy, particularly in college humanities departments, facilitate their welcoming stance not only toward the ethnically diverse but also the exotically cosmopolitan. (A case in point: the CDs purveyed at Starbucks cafés gathering popular music from Brazil to Nepal and beyond.)

This is the class best served by support for the full gamut of cultural expression. The New Class's taste, so varied as perhaps to be incomprehensible as a distinct approach to experience, is a taste nonetheless, the taste for *all of it*. It is well on the way toward becoming the dominant standard of cultural distinction in turn-of-the-millennium America. As this rising class gains power and prestige, the catholicity of its taste becomes acknowledged as the favored cultural stance. And the arts establishment's efforts to enhance the status of and politically gain from alliance with less prestigious social groups fall in nicely with the New Class's marked social tolerance, based on its own varied social origins. Nor would one attentive to ideological stratagems find much for surprise here, since a fair number of arts professionals—such as curators, publicists, editors, and journalists—are themselves members of this class. Without the self-consciousness that has historically led classes to proclaim policies in their own interest, the cultural field is being reoriented in ways that favor the lifestyle and values of an emerging and potentially dominant social group.

NOTES

1. Irving Sandler, *Art of the Postmodern Era: From the Late 1960s to the Early 1990s* (New York, 1996), ch. 13. Confirmation of this account comes with the report that the Bronx Museum of the Arts offers an Artist in the Marketplace program covering topics such as gallery representation, relations with art critics,

marketing, grant writing, public art institutions, museum practices, and tax issues.

2. A substantial volume, *Art in Theory 1900–1990: An Anthology of Changing Ideas*, edited by Charles Harrison and Paul Wood (Oxford and Malden, Mass., 1992), offers programmatic "statements" and interviews from the latter period, poorly matching the copious writing by artists of the earlier period.

3. *Blasted Allegories: An Anthology of Writings by Contemporary Artists*, ed. Brian Wallis (New York, Cambridge, Mass., and London, 1987) makes an effort to bridge this gap between artists and academics, but the contrast in their styles remains marked (Adrian Piper's essay standing out as the exception). Other examples of artists' idealistic but inept esthetics are collected in Bill Beckley and David Shapiro, eds., *Uncontrollable Beauty: Toward a New Aesthetics* (New York, 1998).

4. Written by Gary O. Larson (Washington, 1997). This count liberally includes architects and a "storyteller"; on the other hand, a number of institutional representatives, such as Edward Villela, have been artists in their time.

5. Pierre Bourdieu, *The Field of Cultural Production*, ed. Randal Johnson (New York, 1993); citations that follow are parenthetical.

6. Peter Bürger, *Theory of the Avant-Garde*, trans. Michael Shaw and Jochen Schulte-Sasse (Minneapolis, 1984 [1974]), p. 81.

7. A recent *New York Times* article (Jan. 3, 1999) approvingly recalling the fruitful interaction of black and white musicians in the course of jazz history was greeted with a slew of scornful letters rejecting this discoloration of a racial product. This reaction is apparently more indicative of opinion in the field than the well-meaning efforts in Ken Burns's television series on jazz to credit its widespread sources.

8. Walter Benjamin, "The Work of Art in the Age of Mechanical Reproduction," *Illuminations*, trans. Harry Zohn (New York, 1955); the essay was first published in 1936.

9. Thomas Frank, *The Conquest of Cool: Business Culture, Counterculture, and the Rise of Consumerism* (Chicago and London, 1997).

10. Statements from the initial, entirely political phase of the controversy are assembled in Richard Bolton, ed., *Culture Wars: Documents from the Recent Controversies in the Arts* (New York, 1992).

11. The underlying assumptions of these positions are developed in the essays, particularly one by Kathleen Sullivan on the legal status of free speech restrictions, in Stephen Benedict, ed., *Public Money and the Muse: Essays on Government Funding for the Arts* (New York and London, 1991).

12. See Arjo Klamer, ed., *The Value of Culture: On the Relationship between Economics and the Arts* (Amsterdam, 1996).

13. An instance of this resignation: the theater director and critic Robert Brustein long maintained the view that budget cuts in public support for artistic expression constituted a form of censorship, but in later remarks he granted that this is not literally the case (*The New Republic*, June 1999).

14. *American Canvas*, p. 46; the quotations and data that follow are from this page and p. 42. Subsequent citations are parenthetical.

15. On the early history of the national foundations, see the overview by Milton C. Cummings, Jr. in Benedict, *Public Money and the Muse*, pp. 31–79.

16. The history of this tradition is critically recounted in Alan Swingewood, *The Myth of Mass Culture* (Atlantic Highlands, N.J., 1977). The tradition is not quite dead: Mark C. Miller's *Boxed In: The Culture of TV* (Evanston, Ill., 1988) carries forward the indignation and contempt of the great elitists.

17. Harold Rosenberg, *The Tradition of the New* (New York and Toronto, 1965 [1959]), p. 268.

18. Donald Kuspit, *The New Subjectivism: Art in the 1980s* (Ann Arbor, Mich., and London, 1988), p. 496.

19. The documents, involving Thomas McEvilley, William Rubin, and Kirk Varnedoe, are assembled in Beckley and Shapiro, *Uncontrollable Beauty*, pp. 149–258.

20. Kirk Varnedoe and Adam Gopnik, *High and Low: Modern Art and Popular Culture* (New York, 1990); citations that follow are parenthetical.

21. For the thesis that modernist esthetics enforced this separation and that its dismantling was somehow radical, see Andreas Huyssen, *After the Great Divide: Modernism, Mass Culture, Postmodernism* (Bloomington, Ind., and London, 1986).

22. Charles Rosen and Henri Zerner, *Romanticism and Realism: The Mythology of Nineteenth Century Art* (London and Boston, 1984).

23. The loose correlation of this style, call it postmodernism, with new class taste will be developed in chapter 5.

24. See, for example, Harold Perkin, *The Rise of Professional Society: England since 1880* (London and New York, 1989).

3

Class Amnesia

A Papua New Guinea language has a term for this, *Mokita*. It means "truth that we all know but agree not to talk about."
—Earl Hunt (in *American Scientist*, 1995)

The popular idea that America's is a classless society enjoys a venerable and tenacious history, despite its patent deviation from observable realities.[1] Class may be one of those concepts that members of a community understand very well but tacitly agree to avoid mentioning—a pattern that anthropologists have long studied under the rubric of taboo subjects. The behavior in question also anticipates positive effects, in a form of magic: if social distinctions are avoided in discourse, they will be minimized in practice (if we don't talk about ranks, snobbery and inequality might be lessened). Yet Americans continue to live in distinct neighborhoods (even around the corner from each other), shop in different markets (as well as in the same ones), send their children to different schools (with greater mingling as the grade level rises), and do all the things that rigid class societies are set up to do—only less rigidly.

Since the latter third of the twentieth century, with the handsome success of civil rights legislation in creating minority entrants to the middle class, while leaving a large number of minorities mired in the lower and underclasses, calls for attention to class as well as race and ethnicity have been heard in the land. They are usually framed as a call for economic redress, a demand that smacks of special pleading and has therefore failed to gain wide acceptance. The argument for concern about the divisive role of class has, however, much wider application to social wrongs than exponents of greater equity have urged. Incisive observers such as Benjamin DeMott have made a powerful case against the "myth of classlessness" to expose not only its self-deceptive character but also its insidious political manipulation: "social wrong is accepted in America partly because differences in knowledge of class help to obscure it."[2]

The strong motives that maintain the myth of a classless society in the face of social reality go back to the country's foundations. The constitutional proscription of hereditary titles and privileges is the most visible mark of the antihierarchical principles of the founders, determined to break with the social structure of aristocratic England even while themselves constituting an oligarchy of land and commerce. To this original orientation, the nineteenth century added the liberal ideology of individual enterprise, of the self-made man who could rise in class while thumbing his nose at it. America's populist esprit expressed itself in truculent resistance to esthetic standards that imply cultural hierarchy, even in the period when the crystallization of classes was stimulating differentiation in cultural forms. Profession and practice have repeatedly diverged from each other—a normal environment for the propagation of myths.

But it was only in the twentieth century that hostility to class distinctions passed over into denial of their existence. In the postwar world, a booming manufacturing economy and strong trade unions brought a substantial segment of the blue-collar workforce to home and car ownership and other attributes of middle-class living, with an attendant conception of itself as solidly middle class. The habit spread (statistics to follow), so that by the nineties not only did most Americans think of themselves as middle class but they could be expected to resent inferences that they weren't. In our current political debates, Republican projects (cutting the capital gains tax; flat or flatter tax rates) advertised as for the middle class but clearly favoring the wealthy are met with the Democratic charge of class legislation and the rebuttal that the charge itself encourages class warfare. Why Americans can't think straight about class, indeed, when using the term at all has become a basis for political opprobrium!

Statistical data allowing reflection on this obscurantism may be in order. A *Newsweek*/Roper poll in 1992 revealed a phenomenon that might be called *class conflation*. In this period, at the higher ranges of the income scale, some 30 percent of American families enjoyed incomes of more than $50,000, but only 15 percent of those polled described themselves as upper or upper-middle class. At the same time, whereas 36 percent of U.S. families were to be found in the $25,000–$50,000 income brackets, 57 percent of Americans described themselves as belonging to the middle class. A portion of this "middle" must have been coming from an upper crust chary of identifying itself as such, but a share must be attributed to families making ends meet but inclined to inflate their status. In the lesser ranges of income distribution, a trend toward class inflation is discernible: 21 percent of respondents thought themselves lower-middle class with incomes of $15,000–$25,000, where a sixth of all families fell; another sixth had incomes under $15,000 but only 5 percent of respondents considered themselves lower class. The explanation seems inevitable that people in lower strata tend to inflate their standing, including many claiming to be middle class who are barely equipped to maintain its lifestyle. From both below and above, a disproportionate number of Americans employ the middle-class label to authenticate their membership in the mainstream, while blurring the considerable difference between the living conditions and life expectations permitted to those with incomes of $100,000 (the limit for middle-class comparisons in this report) and to those with a quarter or less of that figure.

A clearer picture of where people actually stand emerges from cost-of-living estimates reported in *The New York Times* in 1998 (July 19): "median household income [is] nearly $40,000, which is enough to live a middle-class life in most of the United States," but "a family of four must bring in at least $27,000 a year from one or more wage earners to maintain . . . 'a minimally adequate standard of living.' " The implication may be drawn that the $40,000 figure is a minimum qualification for middle-class living standards, and those earning between $27,000 and $40,000 constitute the lower-middle class. (Note that in the *Times's* terms, half of all families fall below the middle class's minimum qualification.) Below this range, where "a minimally adequate standard of living" becomes problematic, it is hardly plausible to apply any variant of the term "middle class."[3]

At the higher reaches of the income scale, where lifestyle differences are vigorously acted out and noted, class designations are easier to determine by opinion surveys, although corrections for reality must be made here as well. A *New Yorker*–commissioned survey reported in 1998 (Jan. 5) that the average respondent in a sample representing the "broad masses . . . guesses that a household income of $105,000 a year makes a family upper middle class, that $206,000 makes it upper class, and that fully a quarter of American households fall into each of these categories." According to the Stanford Research Institute, however, only 6.5 percent of families had income in the preceding year more than $100,000 and only 1 percent more than $200,000, so that class inflation persists when estimating elevated as well as middling categories. Yet the income criteria proposed seem fairly well suited to making distinctions at these levels, and plausibly top off the middle class at about $100,000. The upper-middle class may be said to consist of families earning between that figure and $200,000, or some higher limit susceptible to the class position of the estimator. A separate group in the *New Yorker* survey, "college graduates aged between thirty and sixty whose personal (not family) income is more than a hundred thousand dollars a year," proposed $113,000 and $348,000 for upper-middle and upper-class standing, respectively. Although these figures may be distorted by the perhaps overly sensitive judgments this posh group is inclined to make, the first figure does not grossly differ from the more widely held estimate. With the recent stock-market boom and bust, these upper-end criteria become, of course, open to revised estimations.

As the prominent sponsorship of these and similar surveys suggests, the idea of class is alive and well in the practice of economists, marketers, journalists, and the industries they serve. But contemporary discourse, even in these enterprises, avoids the term, favoring "market segments," "socioeconomic status," or "status" *tout court*. The prevailing view is expressed in the heading of a *New York Times Magazine* issue (Nov. 15, 1998) devoted to the subject: "America is a classless society, but every neighborhood, profession and subculture has its pecking order. That means lots of opportunities for prestige . . ."—the latter term being supplanted by "status" throughout the ensuing articles.

A similar shift from socioeconomic to vaguer notions of class has occurred in academic fields, despite the formulaic calls of neo-Marxists on the campuses to keep the idea alive. David Cannadine, a devoted scholar of the history of classes, summarizes the reasons for the change in discourse, especially during the twentieth century's last two decades. They include Marxist sociology's loss of intellectual authority in the wake of communism's widespread breakdown; the strenuous historical research that has complicated the Marxist model of three broad classes and dual class conflicts; the emergence of new occupational groups (such as the New Class) that evade or complicate the standard designations; the influence of "poststructuralism" and related trends that generate skepticism of all "grand historical narratives," with one of which the Marxist concept of class is linked; and the rise of competing interests and preoccupations, so that, for example, "gender has destabilized class as a category of historical analysis."[4] Summing up, Cannadine notes that "Culture now matters more than class" in commanding academic attention.

Yet the existence of class cannot be totally obscured by either a shift toward "status" in journalistic parlance or theoretical shifts in academic research. To cite another scholar's estimation of the data on both past and present classes:

an abundance of evidence for both the nineteenth and twentieth centuries indicates that industrial societies do divide up into broad aggregates of individuals (to use [Max] Weber's cautious and useful phrase) distinguished from each other by inequalities of wealth, income, power, authority, prestige, freedom, life-styles and life chances (to use another of Weber's useful phrases). . . . These aggregates seem to me well described by the term 'class.'[5]

This sociologist studies the still abundant references to and images of class in political, media, and "private, unofficial and popular" discourses, largely but not exclusively in Britain. So perdurable is the traditional explicitness about class distinctions there that the current trend toward class amnesia has yet to prevail. Both Conservative and Labor leaders have mouthed their visions of a classless society, and pundits have attacked the language of class as in itself enforcing snobbery and inequality,[6] but a recognition remains that that ideal state has yet to be achieved.

In some cases, the idea's unfashionable standing has been coolly ignored in impressive scholarly works that make class a continuing research category. To cite one example: Ross McKibbin's *Classes and Cultures: England 1918–1951*[7] is a massive social history that divides into the familiar categories of upper, middle, and working classes. The study concludes, in terms applicable to America as well as Britain: "England had no common culture, rather a set of overlapping cultures. . . . On the whole, people's cultural preferences were self-enclosed and largely determined by class and sex." The field of class discourse is still contested ground, both in America and abroad, at a low intensity level; meanwhile, large numbers of people, if not all, continue to have their lifestyle and life chances defined, if not determined, by their class position.

A metaphysical conundrum that often constrains discussion of class may reasonably be avoided. If, especially among those lower on the scale, more Americans than may plausibly be considered middle class *think* they are, while others avoid the subject on principle or for power, the legendary beast *class consciousness* seems not to stalk this ground. Although shades of Marxism continue to obscure the subject, the study of consciousness has taken forms other than those dreamed of in radical politics. Sociologists have grown accustomed to the elusive existence of groups that demonstrably exist by parameters other than consciousness of themselves as a group. Unlike organizations, which are consciously designed to pursue certain ends, these entities, which bear the unappealing denomination "quasi-groups," are potentially but not necessarily interest- or identity-minded. They are

pluralities of individuals, usually much larger than groups and organizations, who while not organized or structured in interactive systems have through similar situational conditioning acquired similar physical or cultural (ideological, behavioural and technological) or psycholgical characteristics. . . . Examples include humankind, races, nations (as opposed to nation states), ethnic "groups" and classes.[8]

The range of examples may seem to place "class" among a number of very loose categories, but it would take a rash nominalist to decide that these quasi-groups have no real existence. It will also be apparent that quasi-groups' self-consciousness is highly variable, rising and falling over historical time, among classes as well as races and ethnicities.

Key to this as to any formulation of class is the notion of "situational conditioning," a broad rubric covering answers to the implied question, What causes class distinctions? Describing class requires that one enter the theoretical thicket of determining the social forces that make for different situational conditioning. Whereas Marxists limited class formation to the economic realm—the character and relative position of classes being determined by their functional roles in the prevailing system of production—more flexible thinking has expanded the sources of social positioning considerably. Among current social researchers, measuring demonstrable features of "socioeconomic status" is more highly favored than hypothesizing about the sources of class. Yet the parameters employed in discriminating status—at a minimum: income, education, and occupation—may be regarded as causes as well as markers of class. To the Marxist notion of class as determined by occupational and ownership roles within a production and property system—with income an associated differentiating force—contemporary social research adduces education as a key element of class differences. "Educational level attained," a measure of past performance, becomes a continuing influence on occupation and income and, especially in late- or postindustrial society, may be considered the engine of class distinctions. It is also, of course, a lively factor in guiding cultural behavior. Exercising cultural preferences is a normal extension of earlier educational experiences and, far from being an inert reflection of the economic basis of class, lies among its primary constituents. Cultural taste becomes, in this view, an active way of living one's class.[9]

Confirming the role of education in generating contemporary America's social divisions, recent statistics on the upper classes reveal its increasingly salient position. A *New York Times* (Nov. 19, 1995) digest of the evidence on the newly rich and nearly rich yields this datum: among individuals earning more than $100,000 per year—there were already 2.7 million of them by 1993—49 percent had postgraduate or professional degrees. We are witnessing the emergence of a social sector not simply marked by the acculturation acquired in the course of gaining a college diploma but generated by the specialized capacities attained in earning advanced degrees. To the somewhat dry facts that the average income of partners in American law firms was $168,000 in this survey and that of physicians in private practice $218,000 should be added the consideration that incomes of this order open enlarged opportunities for cultural experience, such as travel, acquisition, and charitable investment, to highly educated people. Beyond the sumptuary disparities such rewards create between successful specialists and the rest of society, what subtler changes do these class-distinguishing attributes portend?

Numerous (though not all) members of these and other professions have acquired, in college education and advanced training, a mentality placing a high valuation on expert knowledge. Justifications for this emphasis vary: its purely formal character—knowledge for its own sake; its benefit for individual and social clients; its financial and associated rewards. In a recent summary of this group's attitudes toward knowledge, Steven Brint notes a shift in the professions' service orientation:

Most professionals now justify their work on the basis of its technical complexity, not its social contribution. Professionals are becoming less likely to emphasize selfless service to clients than to emphasize the market demand for expert services. Great emphasis on the ideals surrounding professional activity is prevalent only among the "helping professions" and other professions that have a less secure cognitive authority.[10]

Brint goes on to contrast the relatively conservative politics and pro-business orientation of "expert professionals" with the more liberal views associated with "social trustee professionalism"—the public and non-profit agencies where many remain devoted to the tradition of knowledge for the public good.[11]

To enhance their ability to generate and analyze rarefied knowledge and to design and control pragmatic operations, newer entrants to the professions (and a portion of the already established professionals) have become skilled in manipulating data with computers and associated equipment. It is neither the traditionalist's high valuation on knowledge itself or the more prevalent emphasis on the market value of knowledge, but a complex of attitudes toward and practices in the manipulation of knowledge that marks the emergence of a new grouping within the professions.[12]

These skills in information access, data sharing or "networking" (and data protecting), and in the practical applications of computable knowledge not only enhance the power of this group's expertise but also color the lifestyle choices made possible by its handsome financial rewards. Information technology enables a distinctive approach to thinking and doing in nonoccupational spheres. It is a mental set we may deem a class culture, using the term not only for artifacts and behaviors associated with this grouping but for a view of the world, of what is worthwhile or not in daily living and long-term estimations. A new variety of culture, in this sense, emerged in the wake of the enlargement and transformation of the upper-middle class in late-twentieth-century America. If the group that exhibits these mental and behavioral traits is usefully termed the New Class (a step that requires further justification, which I'll try to provide), its mentality and characteristic practices may be called New Class Culture.

* * *

Ever since Milovan Djilas, a Communist functionary with exemplary vision, defied and defined the Titoist bureaucracy in Yugoslavia, titling his courageous exposé of the mid-fifties *The New Class*, the term has suffered the expected vicissitudes of all broad historical categories—a fate that does not lessen their necessity. In the former Soviet bloc, the category was even conflated with that of the intelligentsia, creating terminological confusion that somehow did not mitigate certain works' considerable descriptive power.[13] In the West, the concept of a new class emerged in tandem with awareness of major changes of structure and operations in the economy and its technology, variously described as late capitalism, the postindustrial economy, or the information society. The term quickly gained political overtones: among the first to employ it in this country, David T. Bazelon made it central to his account of late-sixties radicalism and its prospects.[14] Given their leftist orientation, Bazelon and others were interested mainly in assessing the potential of this emergent class to lead the country in a leftward direction, but irrespective of their ideological designs they made some headway in describing its "culture" (Bazelon's term, on p. 328 and elsewhere). Although this latter was limited to observations that would become clichés—that the phenomenon in question was connected to the growth of suburbia, that it was exemplified in glamorous style by the Kennedys, that it was marked by professionalism, defined as "doing a job well irrespective of its purpose" (p. 326)—a sense of the New Class's social significance began to take hold.

That this significance could be ideological emerged in a stream of articles from the other end of the political spectrum, by Irving Kristol and fellow neoconservatives, which identified the New Class with both sixties-style radicalism and the new moneyed hedonism of the seventies. Although these political caricatures, with either liberal or conservative coloration, have not entirely disappeared, they have given way to more analytic accounts—not all of them in basic agreement yet considerably more enlightening.

For a start, scholars have addressed the implicit question, How new is the New Class? Historians such as Harold Perkin (for England) and Burton J. Bledstein (for America) have documented the long-term growth and current importance of the professions in modern society.[15] Perkin's is perhaps the most sweeping of the accounts of New Class influence, since it makes out professionalized bureaucracy to be all-encompassing and its public administrators to be in a state of civil war with the minions of the private sector—a picture inspired by welfare states such as Britain but probably exaggerated even for those nations.

What emerges more satisfactorily from these studies is the social psychology of a quasi-group elsewhere described mainly in political terms. As Bledstein's title suggests, the growth of a substantial professional element in the middle class brought into being a distinct ethos in vocational and avocational behavior, amounting to the gestation of a new kind of person, a new version of man. These accounts maintain their relevance to late-twentieth-century personality types better than the earlier and more pungent characterizations of postwar large-organization managers, including William Whyte's *Organization Man*, David Riesman's *Lonely Crowd*, and C. Wright Mills's *White Collar*. Eventually the two components, professionals and managers, became closely linked in such schemas as the "professional-managerial class," propounded by Barbara and John Ehrenreich.[16] But the similarity between these subgroups in attitudes toward their hallmark, specialized knowledge, and in cultural behavior has never, to my knowledge, been demonstrated.

At this stage of development in the idea of the New Class, a summary formulation was vouchsafed that became a touchstone for further discussion. Alvin W. Gouldner's *The Future of Intellectuals and the Rise of the New Class*[17] extended left-wing hopes for this grouping, but its lasting importance may lie somewhat to the side of its main thrust. A portion of the not-very-catchy subtitle of the book, "on the Role of Intellectuals and Intelligentsia in the International Class Contest of the Modern Era," indicates both Gouldner's preoccupations and the unexpected consequences of his thinking. Placing himself in the tradition of "left Hegelian sociology" (p. 6), he was interested in the New Class as potentially "the best card that history has presently given us to play" (p. 7), given the failure of the proletariat to fulfill its Marxist destiny. But his examination of this group in terms of the long-standing diad, "intellectuals-intelligentsia," revealed a gap between them that Gouldner aligned with the division between humanistic and technological knowledge workers—his version of the well-worn "two cultures" thesis. This thesis, already hotly debated in the 1940s by C.P. Snow and F.R. Leavis, received a new lease on life in subsequent research showing political and other attitudinal differences between knowledge workers in the public and nonprofit sectors and those in private industry, akin to the differences in work ethos of "social trustee" and "expert" professionals studied by Steven Brint.[18]

At this stage (the late seventies/early eighties), considerable skepticism of the New Class concept was expressed by influential critics. Daniel Bell's "The New Class: A Muddled Concept" and Irving Louis Horowitz's "Is There a New Class?"[19] conveyed withering critiques of the class basis of the concept and of the political implications drawn from it. As the radical aspirations and neoconservative anxieties of earlier decades became muted, however, room was made for less ideological, more concrete observation. Whereas most discussions of the New Class had, with hope or derision, focused on its leftist politics, later studies offered detailed accounts of its occupational varieties, in business, industry, nonprofits, government, et cetera.[20] Meanwhile the actual character of the New Class became clearer in survey research showing it is

not decidedly left-of-center and that professionals in general are in fact moderately conservative on issues having to do with business, labor, and the welfare state. At the same time, professionals are relatively skeptical about moral certainties and tolerant of diversity. They are more liberal on these matters than are other strata in American society. They are, in short, a class in the middle on economic issues, and more liberal than other groups on social relations issues.[21]

Although this research renders earlier political characterizations moot, Gouldner's book remains useful because it takes a measured view of the New Class's capacity to influence other classes by virtue of its elite education, "careful and critical discourse," and more enlightened ethical and social values. Gouldner devotes much of his argument, as every practitioner of "careful and critical discourse" does, to the competing theories of his subject and finds them wanting at precisely this juncture. Considering Talcott Parsons's view of the gradual convergence of the New Class and the "old moneyed" (capitalist) class, with an anticipated uplifting of the latter to form a "new, genteel elite," Gouldner expresses skepticism—not only because capitalists will remain disposed to act strictly on the profit motive but because their expert consultants will be inclined toward the self-assertiveness of any knowledge elite. He makes an incisive interpretation, along the same lines, of the German philosopher Jürgen Habermas's contribution to the subject: Gouldner sees Habermas's account of the "ideal speech community," which could become the arena of genuine democracy, as a surreptitious path along which humanistic intellectuals' ethical values might effectively act upon the technocrats' devotion to efficiency, that is, as an ethical ploy to impose one kind of rationality on another. It is notable that in both these scenarios, the careful and critical discourse of one New Class component is to be deployed for the moral or cultural uplift of either the dominant class or a retrograde portion of its own cohort. Despite his hopes for the progressive influence of the New Class, Gouldner expresses appropriate skepticism of these and other uplifting strategies, particularly Noam Chomsky's romantic-radical version, in which today's intellectuals are found deplorably lacking in high political idealism.

Though there may be ethical uplift to come from the New Class, it will be derived not from its idealism but from the conditions of its members' working lives, habits of mind, educational resources, psychological needs, and existential anxieties—in short, from its culture. Gouldner viewed it as a "flawed universal class" (pp. 7 and 85), speaking both to its international ubiquity in the global economy and to its members' capacity for a cosmopolitan perspective. I shall have more to say of this potentiality in a closing chapter considering the New Class's tendencies toward a cosmopolitan culture, based on its varied ethnic origins and educationally acquired tolerance and receptivity. In the political sphere, it has become clear that the New Class is destined to have no great future as a revolutionary vanguard, but it is also palpable to some observers that "what is shaping up is not a sharpening class war [between the capitalist and New classes] but rather a mutual cultural exchange. The old industrial order is being modified, to some extent 'softened' by the cultural trends of which the new professionals are the principle [sic] carriers."[22] It is this cultural, rather than ethical or political, effect that best represents the New Class's promise of social influence.

The latest version of the New Class thesis has chosen to avoid the troubled term entirely and to invent a new one, "bobos" or bourgeois bohemians, much to the delight of the author's fellow journalists, supplied with a nontechnical, rather cute denomination. David Brooks's *Bobos in Paradise: The New Upper Class and How They Got There*[23] is notable less for its social-scientific acumen (the notion that this "bourgeois" group constitues the upper class, for example) than for its descriptive richness. Wittily detailing the "bohemian" tastes and values of the well educated and newly well-heeled in gentrified inner cities and transformed suburbias, Brooks provides a textured narrative of observable changes in American society that more cautious social scientists have debated with heavy theory and data. (The book also marks a turning in neoconservative circles from an old antipathy to a bemused tolerance toward the now defanged trendy set.) In keeping with survey evidence, Brooks points to the centrality of this group's support for education, especially the education of its own offspring, and its higher degree of tolerance for diversity, which it maintains along with a tendency toward social conservatism (although its bêtes noires are usually on the right). Additional tendencies noted by Brint—commitment to individualism (an "autonomy" at times resembling libertarianism) and "a preference for balancing and synthesizing views on matters of public import" (as Brint puts it, p. 84)—are also adduced in this account of a class culture. Yet the book's indisputable success in highlighting the new environmentalism, the penchant for traditionalist rehabilitation of homes and neighborhoods, and the coffeehouse tastes of this class only sharpens the desire for further behavioral description and finer-grained subjective texture if we are to gain a vivid sense of New Class culture. The need is marked, for this class's culture may prove to be its strongest cohesive feature and its most pervasive form of social influence.

* * *

If the New Class has emerged in late-capitalist or postindustrial civilization as a distinct social entity—a phenomenon on which many observers agree, if only to decry the fact—one would expect its presence to destabilize or reorder not only economic and political relations among the existing classes but also their relative cultural positions. Following Bourdieu's approach, we expect this because cultural preferences convey implications relative to the preferences of others, in keeping with a system of distinctions serving to mark oneself and one's class in an honorific way. Although the existing classes have been content with their more or less enriched cultures, there has usually been resentment and struggle among them, as the opening chapter above recalls. Class cultures have, while changing in content, remained fairly distinct from each other over time, if only to fulfill their differentiating function in the system. And, given the social-psychological and other rewards produced by this structure, one may anticipate that the gratifications offered by higher, middling, and lowly cultures will continue to satisfy the classes associated with them, in varying degrees and with continual modulations. What is new, what is already destabilizing and reordering the structure of cultural distinctions, is the emergence of a new class with new needs among the others.

The historical pattern of emergent classes, so far as it is understood, suggests that such groups quickly develop cultural assets, not only to enjoy within their own spheres but also to declare and bolster their social advent. Aspects of the religious Reformation, of the rise of the novel, and of nineteenth-century realism are examples of cultural developments that are firmly, if not always clearly, linked to the growing importance of the bourgeoisie.[24] Does the emergence of the New Class as yet show cultural innovations that mark it in a like manner? The following chapters will assess contemporary evidence of a distinct behavioral style and attitudinal complex that have been generated by the New Class. But even in the absence of specific artistic styles or media that seem entirely novel ("seem," because historical research invariably links apparent innovations to previous instances, without entirely dissipating their novelty), New Class culture may be seen as distinctive. It might be anticipated that the abruptness of this class's entry into the cultural field would lead it, at least initially, to reorder the relations among existing assets rather than aspire to radical innovation. And this is what we find.

The current consensus in the field of cultural discourse that high-low distinctions in culture are nonexistent or passé or insupportable (the consensus varies to this extent) did not arise at a random moment or place in history but precisely at the point when a new class emerged with distinct sociocultural needs. The historian Michael Kammen has usefully described this consensus in a chapter titled "Blurring the Boundaries Between Taste Levels";[25] reading this, we may be inspired to describe the outcome as the "culture of blurring." As noted above, the New Class is recruited from all classes, on the basis of intelligence, education, and experience, to directly operate or perform professional functions with advanced control technology. Its members do not leave their origins entirely behind but carry varied cultural tastes with them as they enter a social sphere itself in the course of gestation. Heterogeneous cultural traits mingle as New Class members interact with one another, in a process remarkably akin to the classic pattern of ethnic assimilation. As the latter process continues to shape America's social development, the former is proving an equally pronounced shaper of turn-of-the-millennium culture.

The culture of blurring is not, then, merely an intellectual discovery on the part of suddenly and uniformly enlightened cultural leaders but a development with deep roots in a social transformation. The educational sector of the intelligentsia has had a role to play in this development, furthering the New Class's relativistic tendencies by promulgating the values of tolerance and inclusiveness in the humanities and social science courses its members were required to take to supplement their technological training. These values have been well assimilated among the better-educated classes, as indicated by recent surveys,[26] and extend beyond live-and-let-live social attitudes to cultural acceptance and curiosity as well. Just as educational attainment has powered the recruitment and operations of the New Class, achieving a wide range of cultural experience has become a characterizing element, almost a defining requirement, for its members. Culture has not been the determining force in generating the New Class, but its key role in that class's abrupt claim for social recognition has helped to make it highly valued, and to make its spokesmen prominent in the cultural field.

To sense how this influence operates in the prevailing cultural discourse, consider the 1999 two-part exhibition *The American Century* at New York's Whitney Museum of American Art. Now that the enthusiasm for "political correctness" in earlier shows at this and other arts venues has been superseded by more level-headed curatorship, it becomes possible to assess current practice in a balanced way. The exhibition was, by any measure, an impressive summation of a nation's cultural history; I'll avoid promotional terms such as "blockbuster" that have invaded the subfield of museum discourse. Though the triumphant tone of its title and approach—"America takes command," read one heading at the opening of the exhibition's second phase—marked a throwback to a long-eschewed national self-trumpeting, the warts-and-all inclusiveness of its historiography allowed it narrowly to avoid the stigma of jingoism. This inclusiveness is declared as a principle in the museum director's foreword to the first volume of the published catalog: "The history of American art in the first half of this century is in part a history of collapsing boundaries between high art and all that simmered beneath."[27]

In widening its scope, the show surrounded its core display of visual art with examples of contemporary activity in architecture, industrial design, cinema, literature, theater, music, et cetera. The first three of these have already achieved standing in modern art museums, and most of this show's selections would be readily accepted by international observers as examples of outstanding American art. For example, *Citizen Kane* is made much of as a high-water mark film. More popular currents such as film noir and Hollywood musicals are discussed in the catalog in standard generic terms, with instances of esthetic value such as Busby Berkeley dance numbers singled out as transcending run-of-the-mill work. In selecting from allied arts, then, the curators did not glorify popular culture per se but aimed for the highest achievements to be found. No blurring here, merely according esthetic credit where due.

The blurring effect showed itself instead in the treatment of literature and music, where the impulse to be inclusive reveals only amorphousness and condescension. Whereas two major poets, William Carlos Williams and Wallace Stevens, are accorded recognition in a catalog "sidebar" (T.S. Eliot and Ezra Pound—expatriates, to be sure—are mentioned only in passing, mainly for their critical influence), a Nobel Prize–winning novelist, William Faulkner, is dispatched in a single sentence of astonishing puerility. Literature at a different level of artistic authority is, however, accorded ample recognition when it falls under currently approved rubrics of inclusiveness, such as minority group achievement. Thus Zora Neale Hurston and Langston Hughes receive top billing and copious illustration, to the effect that an unsuspecting museum-goer would receive the impression that these were the important writers of the modern period. This distortion is brought on as much by the tenets of cultural blurring as by the imperative to redress past neglect of minorities. Much the same imbalance shows itself in the treatment of music and dance, where jazz is given substantial—though socially rather than musicologically focused—attention while modernist composition goes a-begging. What began as a worthy effort to place visual art in a broad cultural context became vulnerable to the impulses of ideological assertion and cultural leveling.

The American Century may well represent not only the state of the art in museum programming but the state of mind among the classes that sponsor and attend such shows. New Class influence cannot be said to have determined the form and substance of this or any other particular manifestation of artistic taste or expression, but it is difficult to recall a like demonstration in a time before its advent. Nor is it possible to imagine in another country a summation of its artistic achievements that would cast so wide a net: other nations are justly proud to display their folk cultures, but rarely in the same halls and with the same pride as they do their fine arts. The show's self-satisfied assumption of American dominance in the arts and its susceptibility to the ideological shibboleths of the moment reflect the heady economic expansion of the decade, and particularly that of the class largely responsible for technically executing that expansion. Since the culture of blurring accords so well with the New Class's multiple origins and ample resources, we may consider it a distinctive class taste, although it is pleased to call itself a democratic one. We may also conclude that the artistic and critical intelligentsia serving this class, among its primary clients, has muddled an educational responsibility to improve the esthetic acumen of the relatively inexperienced, instead providing a cornucopia of artifacts dashed with dollops of ideological goodwill.

* * *

Though its cultural influence is pervasive, manifesting a distinctive taste in the absence of a specific style, the New Class has had less effect in a related realm, education, where its high level of awareness might have been expected to make a difference. The class inequalities in America's educational system have long been recognized, most sharply since the Coleman Report of 1966 made clear that class-related environment was a determinant of student achievement, shaping attitudes toward teachers, familiarity with learning materials, preschool preparation in language and reasoning, and the study situation as a whole. These implications were updated in 1987 in William Julius Wilson's *The Truly Disadvantaged*, where evidence points to the conclusion that student performance is dependent on variables related to class. Since concerns about the troubled primary and secondary school systems have tended to focus on schools, usually in inner-city neighborhoods, with deficient outcomes, class as well as race has come in for comment; likewise, the class divisions underlying marked differences between urban and suburban schools have gained attention. But in this deeply confused if not traumatized field of discourse, it is not surprising that class-based differentials in learning have failed to gain fuller recognition from scholarly as well as political participants.

The presence of class, particularly the advent of new elements such as the New Class, is more surprisingly ignored in the arena of higher education, where its subtle but continuing influence might have been expected to generate comment. Official discourse in this field maintains a bland obliviousness to unsettling trends beyond the reach of adminstrative action on racial and ethnic balance. A brave effort to get beyond the timely topics to the more fundamental ones is Russell Jacoby's *Dogmatic Wisdom: How the Culture Wars Divert Education and Distract America.*[28] Jacoby notes the uncomfortable common knowledge that educators share: more than half of college students, limited by financial and/or intellectual resources, attend community colleges, whose programs fit them for routinized work rather than for more highly skilled professions; elite institutions still draw their enrollment largely from the upper classes, while making strenuous efforts to leaven it with a respectable proportion of not necessarily underprivileged minorities; the resulting disaggregation of the classes in community and elite institutions (with many intermediate variants, to be sure) tends in the same direction as the public/private, urban/suburban school differences at the earlier levels. Elite school students (minorities included) are being prepared for the professions and the higher business echelons with the special skills that will make them "symbol analysts," solid members of the New Class, whereas a considerable majority are being trained to raise their incomes in respectable middle-class jobs while remaining limited by their class origins and class destinations.

Jacoby's relegation of the "political correctness" controversies to a sideshow has the unfortunate effect, however, of obscuring the troubles within the humanities branch of higher education. The liberal arts are paid intermittent lip service and given occasional special outlays, but are clearly no longer at the center of the academic enterprise and are in greater than ever danger of becoming peripheral. They are, moreover, embarked on internal realignments—interdisciplinary fusions, reorientation toward the arts' sociopolitical context, programs to promulgate women's and minorities' achievements—that, though laudable in their impulses, may prove to be detrimental to their academic standing. The liberal arts are being energetically transformed by numerous humanities professors who regard them, with some justification, as elements of a dominant class's education, for which they are zealous to substitute a less elitist one. That this reformist enterprise of the educators runs counter to the pro-establishment orientation of the New Class's technological wing—Brint's "expert professionals"—has yet to become a sharply focused issue; it has instead raised the ire of classicists and conservatives in the wake of Allan Bloom. The technology- and business-minded, both students and alumni, have been inclined to give the humanists their head while sometimes shaking their own heads in disbelief at the zanier pronouncements, but their tolerance of what many considered to be nonserious matters has begun to show its limits.

Despite the fact that its own origins and future recruitment are so directly affected by the workings of higher education, members of the New Class have by and large taken the route of avoidance behavior. Their selective attention has, however, its brighter side: recent trends in philanthropic activity suggest that this segment of the upper classes is joining others in devoting attention and resources not only to its alma maters but also to the sorry state of primary and secondary education. The multibillion-dollar endowments of the William H. Gates III's foundation on behalf of underprivileged students are being matched, in worthy intentions if not in funding, by those of other nouveau riches in the publishing, cinema, and financial services fields.[29]

More difficult but ultimately more effective than philanthropy alone would be a reorientation in the reigning political ideology, shared by many members of the New Class, that erects redressment of past inequities as the goal of educational initiatives, rather than the nurturing of the best available talent to serve an advanced economy's staffing needs. As a number of observers have contended, the shift of concern, particularly in the Democratic Party, from the working class to racial and other minorities has led not only to a shift of political allegiance among the former group but to disappointing and divisive educational outcomes among the latter.[30] If it is true that a minority-centered orientation contributes to unsettling American education as a whole, it is open to the New Class to help move the nation's political will toward creating primary and secondary systems the equal of those in Japan, Germany, and other nations with advanced technologies, our competitors in the global marketplace. If the laws of class reproduction, by which each generation tries to equip those following with the skills by which they can succeed them, are still operative, it is clearly in the interest of the New Class that American education significantly improve, not only for the benefit of their own offspring but for the nation as a whole, whose long-term primacy depends on such efforts. Already the shortfall in Americans equipped for places in computer-based industries has become acute enough to require exemptions from immigration quotas to allow staffing by foreign workers. If and when the New Class moves toward taking a leadership role in this realm, it will have begun to assert itself as a leading social force.

* * *

Where does the New Class stand at present? A sure sign both that such a group formation actually exists and that it is acquiring a degree of prominence is the new form of disdain accorded it by influential pundits, now that its radicalism has become a stale canard. The most systematic denigration of this grouping (although it avoids the class designation) came in a series of books by Christopher Lasch, beginning with a denunciation of its affluent hedonism in *The Culture of Narcissism* (1978), showing greater sympathy with its psychic anxieties in *The Minimal Self* (1984), and reaching a populist condemnation of its self-distancing from other classes in *The Revolt of the Elites and the Betrayal of Democracy* (1995). A yet more vitriolic populism appeared in the latter year in Michael Lind's *Next American Nation*, where an "overclass" of executives, professionals, and rentiers became the enemy. Here this catch-all grouping was scorned not merely for its financial success but specifically for its educational advantages ("most of them with advanced degrees").[31]

These charges were made explicit in an opinion piece by former *New York Times* editor Max Frankel, which, citing data on the increasing income gap among the classes, places blame not only on computers as such but also on the experts who control them: "Computers have enriched a small class of technological wizards and management consultants who streamline production. . . . But those same computers have eliminated many jobs and significantly reduced the skills needed in the jobs that survive, thereby weakening the bargaining power and income of most wage earners."[32] Responses of this kind to the transformations that increased national productivity and widespread prosperity in the 1990s—and that despite a lapse into recession are being sustained at historically high levels—can only be described as Luddite, and the populist scorn of an elite with advanced degrees represents an updated version of a long-standing anti-intellectual tradition.

More probing of the deeper social consequences of the New Class's emergence (here, too, without naming the class as such) was Daniel Bell's *Cultural Contradictions of Capitalism* (1976). The chief contradiction in question was this: that the economy still requires of its workers an internalization of restraint—the "Protestant ethic" of Weber and Tawney, a self-discipline that promotes saving and investment as well as workplace efficiency—whereas the consumer orientation of modern capitalism encourages spirited if not hedonist consumption, extending beyond buying habits to other forms of behavior. Bell's observation of this paradox was, of course, made in response to the explosion of self-expression and self-indulgence in the sixties and seventies; in the closing decades of the century, the mix of technological efficiency and lavish consumerism came to seem not merely noncontradictory but a normal interdependence, like previous enhancements of lower- and middle-class buying power, one that was good for the economy.

Yet Bell's insight helps to clarify a source of resistance to the New Class's advent: not middle- or lower-class resentment of its higher wages and glitzy lifestyle (which has yet to become articulate), but intellectuals' resentment of its competition for cultural leadership. Although the two groupings are partially overlapping—some members of the intelligentsia having achieved New Class technical expertise and corresponding in-comes—in most contexts the two remain distinct. The intellectual tradi-tion of disinterested inquiry and selfless devotion to truth, though it is perhaps in decline of late, calls for associated forms of self-management of the kind sacred to the Protestant work ethic. Many members of the New Class, on the other hand, employ their enriched educational back-ground and handsome income not in the older forms of high living but in a carefree cultural adventurousness that seems to belie the seriousness of the arts they explore and exploit. Or at least that is the rationale that some intellectuals give to their resentment of these new entrants in the cultural field.

The following chapters will try to describe these nuanced behavior patterns, arriving at the titular subject of this book, "New Class culture"; at this point, my account of new relations between the classes may con-clude on a more limited subject. The American intelligentsia, a significant portion of which sustains the honorable tradition of democratic egalitar-ianism, will inevitably display discomfort with cultural objects and events designed to cater to an elite. The New Class's omnivorousness sweeps up many an artifact and performance not so designed, but its intense cultural curiosity, backed by ample financial resources, must present a troubling spectacle to traditional intellectuals of more Spartan bearing. The recent and still roiling culture wars may have their source in differences of temperament not more august than these. Preferring to speak for and counsel the minority groups that have made impressive claims for their cultural dignity as well as their civil rights, the intelli-gentsia has chosen to neglect—when it has not disdained—the more successful rising class of highly educated, but culturally somewhat in-experienced, professionals. Although the left-wing intellectual contingent must by now be disabused of any hopes it once harbored of guiding the New Class's revolutionary potential, it is not too late for them and others to play a more appropriate and more sustainable cultural leadership role.

This class, which came into being by the power of education, still needs educating in its own cultural values and in its responsibilities as a leading, perhaps ultimately dominant, social group. Vast outputs of museum displays, artistic performances, book and magazine publications, and so on are being generated to tap this fertile market. A rise in quality as well as quantity of cultural activity might well result from a conscious effort by the intelligentsia to assess the New Class as a rising group that stands in need of guidance. A segment of the intel-ligentsia has in recent decades savored the self-image, set for it by the Marxist theoretician Antonio Gramsci, of "organic intellectuals," guiding spirits to a rising class—still, alas, attaching itself to classes, whether the proletariat or the minority underclass, that failed to arise. It is open to the intelligentsia to be the organic intellectuals of a demonstrably rising class, acting as cultural rather than political guides. But it must first, of course, establish its authority on firmer ground than that promoted by the culture of blurring, in which no authority is allowed to stand.

NOTES

1. What constitutes observable reality is, to be sure, a highly debatable concept. The latest and most formidable refutation of the idea that America's is a class society, Paul W. Kingston's *The Classless Society* (Stanford, Calif., 2000), vaunts its commitment to objective measurement, yet falls short even within its principled positivism. Its argument is, indeed, sober and amply supported by statistical data; I shall leave it to heavier sociological hitters (whose works are summarized in the opening chapter) to argue their proper interpretation. To restrict my cavils to Kingston's treatment of class culture (the subject to be pursued here): his focus is on cultural indices other than esthetic taste. Although data on parenting patterns and moral attitudes may be favored by social scientists pursuing good numbers on human behavior, they do not comport well with people's preferences in the arts. When Kingston does offer data on "Class and the Arts" (p. 134), he acknowledges that "some small segments of the economic and academic elites have a distinctive taste for classical music," et cetera, but minimizes this correlation: "only a small proportion [of these elites] . . . actively consumes these 'elite' art forms" (p. 136). The significance of this point is made moot by the absence of statistics to support it, in contrast to the labored documentation of almost all other statements in the book. When addressing the theoretical basis of the "class culture" idea, Kingston's account of Bourdieu follows the familiar form of American scientistic disdain for Continental speculation and prose style (p. 123), while refraining from discussion of the massive survey data in Bourdieu's *Distinction*. Although *The Classless Society* marks a substantial contribution to the study of class theory and analysis, it is far from settling the issues it so industriously engages.

2. Benjamin DeMott, *The Imperial Middle: Why Americans Can't Think Straight about Class* (New York, 1990), pp. 10–11. For a full statistical accounting of these wrongs, including increasing income and wealth inequality, poverty among working families, and denigration of the structurally poor as a "welfare class," see Mark Zweig, *The Working Class Majority: America's Best Kept Secret* (Ithaca, N.Y., and London, 2000), chs. 3–4.

3. I cite these income and cost-of-living statistics to make a broad estimate of class distinctions in daily living; educational and occupational factors are also relevant and will be employed below. Another approach to defining class, based on autonomy or lack of it in the workplace, that is, "power," is ingeniously devised in Zweig, *The Working Class Majority*, ch. 1; his analysis of census data differentiates middle- and working-class components within various occupational categories—for example, "sales" and "services"—in an arguable but inevitably contestable way.

4. David Cannadine, *The Rise and Fall of Class in Britain* (New York, 1999), pp. 8–15.

5. Arthur Marwick, introduction to Marwick, ed., *Class in the Twentieth Century* (Brighton, U.K., 1986), pp. 3–4.

6. See P.N. Furbank, *Unholy Pleasure, or The Idea of Social Class* (Oxford, 1985).

7. Ross McKibbin, *Classes and Cultures: England 1918–1951*, (Oxford, 1998); the quotation that follows is from p. 527.

8. Brian K. Taylor, introduction to Taylor, ed., *Race, Nation, Ethnos and Class: Quasi-Groups and Society* (Brighton, U.K., 1996), p. 4. Taylor cites a succession of sociologists who have described class in similar terms.

9. In *Distinction* and elsewhere, Pierre Bourdieu's concept of *habitus* describes the totality of class-bound lifestyles and thought patterns.

10. Steven Brint, *In an Age of Experts: The Changing Role of Professionals in Politics and Public Life* (Princeton, N.J., 1994), p. 82. Among the "helping professions," physicians, with their considerably higher reward structure, are an obviously complex case.

11. An implication drawn by Brint may be challenged here: following conservative characterizations, he understands the New Class as a professional grouping with liberal-to-radical social and political attitudes. Since "expert professionals" don't markedly maintain these attitudes, this cluster is confined at most to "social trustee professionals," where its importance may be minimized. In my view, which doesn't assume New Class leftism, it includes members of both types, insofar as they exhibit working and cultural practices closely related to the new technology.

12. Other observers have focused on one or another feature of the new mentality of this class: for Peter L. Berger, secular humanism ("The Worldview of the New Class: Secularity and its Discontents," in B. Bruce-Briggs, ed., *The New Class?* [New Brunswick, N.J., 1979]); for Daniel Bell, modernist attitudes, constituting it as a "mentality, not a class" ("The New Class: A Muddled Concept," also in the Bruce-Briggs collection); for Alvin W. Gouldner, its "careful and critical discourse" (*The Future of Intellectuals and the Rise of the New Class* [New York, 1979]). These and other characterizations will be discussed below.

13. See George Konrad and Ivan Szelenyi, *The Intellectuals on the Road to Class Power*, trans. Andrew Arato and R.E. Allen (New York and London, 1979). The term for the Eastern European grouping that eventually emerged as the favored and appropriate one is the Russian neologism *nomenklatura*—that is, those with names and titles in a bureaucratic hierarchy.

14. David T. Bazelon, *Power in America: The Politics of the New Class* (New York, 1967); cited parenthetically afterward.

15. Harold Perkin, *The Rise of Professional Society: England since 1880* (London and New York, 1989); Burton J. Bledstein, *The Culture of Professionalism: The Middle Class and the Development of Higher Education in America* (New York, 1976).

16. Barbara and John Ehrenreich, "The Professional-Managerial Class," in Pat Walker, ed., *Between Capital and Labor* (Boston, 1979), pp. 12–27.

17. Gouldner, *The Future of Intellectuals and the Rise of the New Class*. Citations that follow are parenthetical.

18. A summary of research on the gap within the professions is given by Brint: "Specialists in the civic sphere, in social relations, and culture—academics, artists, journalists, policy specialists, social scientists—are a relatively liberal segment of the professional stratum. Even this liberal segment, however, shows a conservative profile on issues involving labor, welfare, the reduction of income inequalities, and crime control" (*In an Age of Experts*, p. 87). Studies of academic

opinion conducted over the years by Seymour Martin Lipset (for example, his contribution to the Bruce-Briggs essay collection cited above) tend to confirm this disparity by showing a similar gap between the professoriate and other professionals, while closer examination reveals that left-wing attitudes are prominent only in a limited number of academic fields, primarily the humanities and social sciences, although not predominant even there.

19. Daniel Bell, "The New Class: A Muddled Concept," in Bruce-Briggs, *The New Class?*; Irving Louis Horowitz, "Is There a New Class?" in *Society* 16 (1979), no. 2.

20. See Hansfried Kellner and Frank W. Heuberger, eds., *Hidden Technocrats: The New Class and New Capitalism* (New Brunswick, N.J., and London, 1992).

21. Brint, *In an Age of Experts*, pp. 85–86.

22. Kellner and Heuberger, *Hidden Technocrats*, p. 19.

23. David Brooks, *Bobos in Paradise: The New Upper Class and How They Got There* (New York, 2000).

24. The subject is a contentious one and has yet to emerge from the shadows cast by Marxism, but it's hard to conceive of a sociology of art without such assumptions. Scholars even in the Marxist tradition, such as Arnold Hauser and Lucien Goldmann, have considerably refined art's class correlations, whereas those outside it, like Ian Watt and Diana Spearman, have made them more precisely applicable to specific arts—in their case, to the rise of the novel.

25. Michael Kammen, "Blurring the Boundaries Between Taste levels," *American Culture/American Tastes: Social Change and the 20th Century* (New York, 1999), ch. 5.

26. For example, Alan Wolfe, *One Nation, After All: What Middle-Class Americans Really Think . . .* (New York, 1998).

27. Maxwell L. Anderson, in Barbara Haskell, *The American Century: Art and Culture 1900–1950* (New York and London, 1999), p. 9.

28. Russell Jacoby, *Dogmatic Wisdom: How the Culture Wars Divert Education and Distract America* (New York, 1994).

29. *New York Times*, Sept. 23, 1999; the big donors representative of these fields are, respectively, Leonard Riggio (of Barnes & Noble), George Lucas, and Eli Broad.

30. Richard D. Kahlenberg, *The Remedy: Class, Race, and Affirmative Action* (New York, 1996); see also Mickey Kaus, *The End of Equality* (New York, 1992).

31. Michael Lind, *The Next American Nation: The New Nationalism and the Fourth American Revolution* (New York, 1995), p. 99.

32. Max Frankel, "Do Computers Eat Our Paychecks?" *New York Times Magazine*, March 10, 1996.

4

New Class Mentality

Wired is about the most powerful people on the planet today.
—Louis Rossetto, its publisher

A young man sits with a laptop computer across the aisle from me on an Amtrak train, working on what appears to be a school assignment. After diligent efforts in this direction, energy flags; he inserts a digital videodisc in a side port and watches a recent movie—*Pleasantville*, as it happens, which employs digital techniques to mix color with black-and-white images for its narrative system. Meanwhile, the young woman seated with him reads with evident satisfaction a paperback book, mile after mile, hour after hour. Her attention, too, lapses and she uses her cellular phone for a friendly chat. Observing them discreetly, I'm aware that nothing spectacular is happening here, but the thought arises that this lack of strangeness is itself part of the spectacle. I, too, could be similarly equipped and employed, though I'm not, so that the distance across the aisle represents not a generational but a cultural difference. It is clear to me and, when I ask the fellow some questions about his apparatus, probably to them that we are very different from each other, though we're together in a "business class" car and are college-educated all. I feel an impulse, perhaps experienced by others of my background, to wonder: Who are these people and what do they want?

A fog of journalese surrounds this, like other newly emergent groups: "baby boomers," "yuppies," and "Generation X" have had their day as cutting-edge slang but still linger in the ether. Such terms respond to evident distinguishing features such as age, diction, and dress style, but fail at deeper characterization. More salient than these attributes of the young people beside me is their relationship to machines, their easy familiarity with and utter lack of awe at the powers under their command. One is also struck by their additional capacity and inclination, lacking in other segments of their age cohort, to read books. Beyond their skill in accessing information in up-to-date ways, they retain an investment in and respect for the older ones. (Any doubts of this are dispelled by surveying the array of computer books in your neighborhood mega-bookstore.)

A sociological assessment of these young people's class position would require data on their education, occupation (or training program), and income or expectations, but it is already clear that they are masters, if not yet of the universe, then of some of the most advanced techniques for dealing with certain kinds of reality. They are, in short, controllers. Already at this stage of their lives controlling sophisticated communication, information, and entertainment resources, they will eventually be able to control production and supply flows, design of new equipment and building projects, marketing, and information distribution. Every society has its technology and the administrators of that technology; these are the controllers for our time.

"Control" is, of course, a dirty word in certain cultural lexicons. For libertarians of the right and left, it is the enemy, and every time these individualists buy mass-produced goods or watch mainstream television or movies they must deal with the unhappy consciousness of being at least partially controlled by large-scale human processing systems. "Control" is, on the other hand, a synonym for key elements of civilization, as in "control of the environment" or "self-control." The history of control systems—James R. Beniger's *The Control Revolution*[1] is the most substantial known to me—reads very much like a history of the world from the discovery of writing (linked to the recording of agricultural stores) to our present pass. Machines for regulating, enumerating, and modifying the production and distribution of goods and services are, however much we may incline to think first of Bach or Shakespeare, the leading features in determining human progress, measured in such terms as health, life expectancy, wealth, productivity, literacy, educational quantity if not quality, and population growth—the social and biological measures of species success.[2] The humble steam-pressure gauge and textile loom card have had as much to do with our becoming civil and happy (to the extent we are so) as have Bach and Shakespeare. And those who devise and maintain these controls are likewise our benefactors, demanding similar acknowledgment and appreciation.

The group of workers called into existence to plan and oversee modern control systems might, in dystopian fiction and classic films, have been called "controllers."[3] "Professional-managerial class" conveys a more neutral view, considering that the world has not become the dictatorial technocracy once feared, and still envisaged in popular media. But this term, too, when applied to the entire range of professionals and managers, fails to render the specific input of these controllers. Computers are employed in almost all professions and managements, but not all professionals and managers control and operate them, beneficiaries though they may be. An anecdote may perhaps make the distinction clearer than would massive data: an acquaintance of mine, a multiply skilled lawyer, is distinguished in her international marketing firm by the tag, "She's the one who makes the computers work for us." It is this controlling group within the professions, business, government, and industry that has emerged with New Class status and potential power.

It is important to maintain this distinction if the frequently employed term "knowledge workers" is not to become yet another journalistic sobriquet.[4] The "knowledge economy" was the economist Fritz Machlup's term for the five categories of activity—education, research and development, communications media, information machines, and information services—that have come to generate the major portion of the gross national product. Although those employed in these activities might with some latitude be called "knowledge workers," not all can be counted among the New Class, since they include large numbers of clerical, manual, sales, and other controlled but not controlling personnel. The proportion of controllers to other roles probably resembles that in higher education, where a relatively small cadre of professors and research directors is accompanied by numerous technicians, administrative staff, maintenance workers, and the like. Even within the business stratum that controls production, distribution, and other activities by manipulating data, differences exist between those employing the latest technology and those relying on earlier modes of memory retrieval, assessment, and application. Although it would no doubt be invidious to propose strict standards for New Class entry on the basis of computer familiarity, any comparison between erstwhile captains of industry, doctors, lawyers, or members of the intelligentsia and the present crop would have to take account of this, the major difference in their means of doing business. That difference lies at the origin of the New Class's social emergence.

* * *

To this point, I have directed attention to the new technological roles and changed work patterns that account for the New Class's advent. A growing fund of commentary now allows for a few generalizations on the social-psychological character of its members. Since most observers emphasize the novelty of this personality type (and the novelty of their own insights), it is important to gain historical perspective in considering its degree of uniqueness. A number of historians have remarked on the spread of an elevated ethos among the American middle classes in this century, a code of well-bred and reasonable self-restraint often scornfully targeted as "middle-class morality" by those claiming a still higher spirituality. Peter N. Stearns has, in addition, singled out a psychological component of this behavioral style, calling it, in a book with the phrase for its title, "American cool."[5] A consistent theme of these studies is that as prosperity spreads in this century beyond an ancestral elite, the latter's norms of genteel conduct and refined taste spread with it. Another implication is that along with standards of value and conduct—it is hard to tell whether as cause or effect—go emotional changes, inner responses that make up what Raymond Williams has called a "structure of feeling." The cultivated habits of cool detachment and reserved judgment, though not uniformly maintained throughout the middle classes, nor consistently even among its cooler individuals, may be seen as preparing the ground for the end-of-the-century developments that are our subject.

The traits of postwar, or postsixties, personality and behavior are frequently said to include the following: loss of a sense of the past or regulative tradition; diminished empathy or, reciprocally, heightened self-centeredness; avoidance of inwardness as conveyed in art and personal relations, that is, a preference for surface over depth in vision and feeling; et cetera. These traits, collectively referred to as "decenteredness," have been much remarked upon by left-leaning social critics such as Fredric Jameson, David Harvey, and Marshall Berman as indicating another of the human deficiencies of capitalism. While at times negotiating a ticklish course between ideological censoriousness toward and personal participation in the new structure of feeling, these critics have usefully expanded our sense of the subjective quality of this decenteredness. Disdaining "current fantasies about the salvational nature of high technology," Jameson points out that "postmodern hyperspace . . . has finally succeeded in transcending the capacities of the individual human body to locate itself, to organize its immediate surroundings perceptually, and cognitively to map its position in a mappable external world."[6]

One need not be a Marxist, conflicted or otherwise, to paint the newly forming social type in somber tones. In the fifties, with the prominence of William Whyte's "organization man" and David Riesman's "other-directed" business personality, social scientists were attentive to both the disorienting and the compensatory self-disciplining consequences of capitalism's expansion in scale and bureaucratic complexity. The psychic costs of this self-regulation seem to have been considerable, and are considered—in the formula, a revolt against the fifties—to have helped provoke the widespread social upheavals of the sixties. But changes in the workings of capitalism, particularly the rise of an information economy, moved toward the making of a new kind of worker in knowledge-based industries, with a concomitant shift in social attitudes and personal behavior. It is of these shifts that more recent theories of the New Class have striven to keep abreast.

Francis Fukuyama, in his complacent account of the post–cold war "end of history," suggested that the triumphant capitalist economy and technology were sources of benign conflict resolution, if not of universal happiness. Yet he more recently joins other conservative social critics in painting American attitudes and behavior in a rueful picture of what he calls the "Great Disruption."[7] It includes rising rates of divorce and out-of-wedlock childbirth (usually associated with the underclass but observable also in more elevated groupings); higher levels of social distrust, toward both public entities and private relationships; and increasingly individualistic attitudes and behavior in social contexts (nicknamed, after R.D. Putnam's much-debated thesis, "bowling alone"), attitudes also expressed in the political sphere. Though Fukuyama avoids the moralistic use of such data by holding out hope for evolutionary resources that might bring about a recentering, he provides grounds for the apocalyptic predictions of futurologists such as Alvin Toffler, for whom the information age will bring a disuniting of society by encouraging decentralization, demassification (through special provisions for the elite), and desynchronization (when business and other activities run without real-time constraints).[8] Yet any futurologist can make a mistake, and conservative applications of devolutionary doctrine, exhibiting both alarm at the purported decline in social responsibility and a perhaps inconsistent libertarianism, at least in the economic sphere, have come to seem starry—or is it bleary?—eyed.

* * *

What can be said about the ongoing reshaping of the American mentality—and of the New Class among its prominent components—that would avoid the alarmist strictures of both leftist and conservative social critics? We may take a cue from one of the foremost shapers of a new consciousness, William Gibson, the author of the futuristic and dystopian *Neuromancer* (1984), who coined the word "cyberspace" to describe a realm of "consensual hallucination."[9] Gibson clearly stated his position in a *New York Times Magazine* piece (July 14, 1996) titled, "The [Inter]Net is a Waste of Time and that's exactly what's right about it." Without joining this fantasist in his ruminations on a favored form of relaxation, one senses that the new technologies are not all business and meaningful communication. The element of play is surely one of the characterizing aspects of any cultural epoch, and we may be closer to the current struc-

ture of feeling when attentive to New Class forms of play than in check-
ing on its more sober performances. What makes the ludic dimension of
Internet use particularly appealing for this grouping is the continuity
between work and play it offers: these masters of control are disposed
to use the same technology that got them there in after-hours activities
such as games, electronic doodling, and various forms of commercial
entertainment. To pin a phrase on this disinterested and mainly benign
behavior pattern, perhaps "computerized relaxation" may serve.

A related characteristic that calls for singling out is the propensity of
members of this class to conduct much of their social life through the
computer. Beyond the one-to-one contacts people make through e-mail,
beyond the multiple pronouncements they are capable of through off-
line circuits and mailing lists, they richly indulge in interactive groups
called MUDs, multi-user domains, or MUGs, Macintosh user groups.
These ethereal associations have been recommended, as one handbook
puts it, for getting "your social cravings slaked," but the claims for and,
apparently, the rewards of this resource go well beyond the pleasures of
schmoozing. One prominent guru, Howard Rheingold, projects these activities as a new mode of political association, one that Tocqueville never
dreamed of but that he might well have recognized as a very American
phenomenon (though by now it's worldwide). Rheingold's title, *The Virtual Community: Homesteading on the Electronic Frontier*,[10] reveals much
about the political mentality in question: the book describes the Whole
Earth 'Lectronic Link (WELL), a computer conferencing system that allows widely scattered groups to carry on public meetings. Such groups
have formed regionally (apparently with great success in the San Fran-
cisco Bay area), nationally, and internationally to offer mutual support
("communion"), exchange information (often scientific and otherwise
recondite), and "socially network" on behalf of environmental and other
social goals. Although the guru's suggestions that these interactions constitute a "virtual village" or "small town" meeting are metaphorical if
not mythological, it's also clear that his designation of them as a "grassroots use of technology" has something to be said for it. To technological
relaxation, we may add "electronic socializing" as a characteristic New
Class behavior pattern.

Since much communication—verbal and nonverbal, even at a distance—has a sexual component, we would expect that the realm of the
erotic life has also been affected by new patterns of social and recreational activity. That these effects take place not only unconsciously, as
an epiphenomenon of the apparatus itself, but also with great determination and investment has been attested by experts in the matter such
as Sherry Turkle. Her *Life on the Screen: Identity in the Age of the Internet*[11]
provides fulsome accounts of the more explicit channels of the new sexuality: role playing, including sex switching, by e-mail; computer therapy

programs for psychic disorders; virtual reality provisions of orgasmic experience (much hyped but apparently still in the experimental stage). These are among the more literal expressions of the new sexuality; there is a broader sense in which the technology itself is erotically charged, de rigueur for acceptability in chosen circles, *with it* (as opposed to the impotent and intolerable "without it").

Given these abundant resources for diversion, action, and expression, the New Class—along with others who are willing and able to make use of them—is inclined to join technology exponents in hailing its encouragement of possibility, creativity, and freedom. Accompanying this optimistic, at times utopian, treble is a somber, at times depressive, ground bass. The World Wide Web, we are told, is a lonely planet: the actual as opposed to virtual reality is that of youngish people seated in solitude at keyboard and screen, interacting fast and furiously but confined to the space of and around their own bodies. A typical report of one such study (*New York Times*, Aug. 30, 1998) is titled, "Sad, Lonely World Discovered in Cyberspace." Accounts of the loneliness of the long-distance socializer, lacking face-to-face personal engagement and other inducements to genuine communion are rife, though perhaps overly solicitous.[12] There is evidence that people who work long hours on the Internet become susceptible to a range of physical and psychic illnesses, but the frequency and depth of these effects have yet to reach epidemic scale.

Lamentations over the baleful consequences of the wired life read between the lines as responses to more widespread social deficiencies such as the loss of community (by certain analysts' measures) and the anxieties of modern or postmodern existence (according to others). The French sociologist Jean Baudrillard became something of a technology guru by offering a double vision of this form of existence: both its delirious power to call up images never seen on land or sea ("simulacra"), mix and modify materials in all media, and stimulate individual and group imagination; and its soul-constricting superficiality, anxiety-provoking isolation, and ultimately despairing barrenness.[13] Add to these diffuse reactions the more specific anxieties associated with the anonymity provided, for good or ill, by electronic messages, the threats and promises of data encryption, and the sheer volume of data accessed and accessible, and we recognize the latest version of the Faustian bargain that mankind has made with technological progress across the centuries. Although the computer may be contributing to this malaise, its removal or limitation (even if possible) could not be expected to heal it.

Another consequence of everyday computer usage by the New Class and others is the promotion of cultural forms that have been labeled "cyberculture" but may also be considered "digitalized escapism." Mark Dery's *Escape Velocity: Cyberculture at the End of the Century*[14] describes a long string of escapist activities: New Age programs of "consciousness technology" providing therapy and quasi-religious spirituality; "underground roboticists" and cybernetic body artists projecting fusions of man and machine or offering to enhance the physiological with the mechanical; "RoboCopulation" or advanced versions of the generalized eroticism indicated above; prophetic minimovements questing for posthuman evolution, a way out of history and earthly gravity, contact with extraterrestrials, or achievement of immortality. How many members of the New Class tap into these Web sites, how many believe any or all of this farrago, remains unclear, but their observable curiosity about quasi-esthetic, imaginative, and arcane psychic phenomena suggests that a substantial number are pursuing Internet searches for information that transcends the practical.

Linked to the proliferation of "wired" cultural activities is a linguistic phenomenon that has been termed "technobabble."[15] It may be reckoned a form of the entropy or noise associated with all information systems, but bearing the marks of this system's associations with engineering and with commerce. John Barry provides a solid but inevitably satiric account of this cultural discourse. Like other jargons, this one is called into being by new activities and, on the positive side, makes for fresh recognition of new phenomena. Along with clumsy abstractions ("to interface," "to network"), it includes pithy metaphors ("bug," "virus") and stark polar terms ("hackers" and "losers"). Barry also collects samples of less salutary linguistic behavior: usages that are mere filler or decoration, terms employed for obfuscation or cover-up, obsessive enunciation (or pathological technobabble), and usage "by those unfamiliar with its meanings in an attempt to sound as if they know what they are talking about." Among the dysfunctions associated with this, as with any, communications system, technobabble distorts the psychic and social reality of both its speakers and their interlocutors. With patronizing and deceptive locutions in marketing and public relations ("user-friendly," "client and server"), it fosters an illusion of innocent social practice. And its metaphoric diction stimulates dreams of unlimited possibility: the brain as hardware, working on information as software, "browsing" or "surfing" in an infinite medium.

* * *

The potentialities opened up by computers may eventually redound to the benefit of all mankind, but those first in line to become aware of and to tap them, even to become intoxicated with them, are the "hackers," to employ the technobabble term. As a subgroup within the New Class, these technical specialists—programmers, problem solvers, data-security protectors, et cetera—share the broad characteristics outlined above, yet are distinguished by a more marked dedication to the control machinery itself. Although researchers, marketers, financial planners, et al. use the computer with aplomb, they do so instrumentally in pursuing their primary goals; for hackers, the computer is itself the primary interest. It would be caricatural to describe this occupational grouping in personal or cultural terms: how many traits do the programmers of Bangalore, India, recently requisitioned by American firms share (as yet) with their new colleagues in Silicon Valley or Route 128? Although their physiognomies and lifestyles vary as widely as the world, hackers perceptibly cluster at one end of the human distribution of at least one key attribute: intelligence.

Even to call up the image of the bell curve, as the preceding sentence does, is to inspire unease in many and hostility in some; the psychology and sociology of intelligence as a factor in human relations and social stratification has become, when not a taboo subject, a field for vilification and hysteria. (Not only the bien-pensant left but a self-critical liberal journal, *The New Republic*, joined in this hue and cry: its open-mindedness allowed it to publish a coauthor's summary of *The Bell Curve*, but it preceded the article with a raft of denunciations by its editors and others, as if to cushion the inevitable shock and outrage.) Yet the long devotion and important contributions of Richard J. Herrnstein, the book's coauthor, now deceased, to the study and elucidation of this psychophysical reality cannot, despite the concerted opprobrium directed against him from the outset,[16] be relegated to obscurity, whatever the political cut-and-thrust engendered by and directed against its other author, political scientist Charles Murray. The primary subject of *The Bell Curve* is not, as its detractors imply by their exclusive attention, its (in)famous Part 3 on ethnic and racial differences in intelligence testing (especially the perdurable performance of African-Americans at more than one standard deviation—equivalent to some sixteen IQ points—below the mean for whites) and the correlation of these differences with poverty, crime, and other deplorable social facts, but the larger issues evoked by its subtitle: *Intelligence and Class Structure in American Life.*[17]

In the perspective that emerges from reading *The Bell Curve* by engaging with its developing argument, rather than from a prepared resistance to all descriptions of racial disparities, the true subject of the book is not African-Americans but the New Class. Its account of the difference that intelligence makes in educational levels, income, and other constituents of class highlights the emergence of the highly intelligent and better educated to prominence in a knowledge-based economy and consequently to increasing power in other channels of social life. The book's implications for the future course of social relations between this group and others may be even more unsettling than its skepticism about the efficacy of educational and other efforts to ameliorate the condition of those at the lower end of the intelligence and class scales. *The Bell Curve* is indeed a disturbing book, in its confirmation of the speculative trends drama-tized in that dystopian classic on the triumph of (and rebellion against) the New Class, Michael Young's *Rise of the Meritocracy: 1870–2033*.[18]

By dint of the social-psychological phenomenon called "assortative mating"—a scientific concept confirming everyday observation—people of similar intelligence levels tend to select each other out and thereby reinforce, both genetically and culturally, the continuation of their kind. Thus the New Class not only reproduces itself by providing select edu-cation for its offspring, like other advantaged groups, but encourages professional and technological training in a more methodical and con-sistent way than other classes do. This manner of passing on what can only be considered a form of wealth—educational capital, as sociologists like Bourdieu would call it—serves in much the way inherited property has done historically to maintain the dominant position of ruling classes. We are here faced with a vision of the future at least as distressing as that of a society permanently riven by racial differences. It is a vision that underlies the frequent use of "meritocracy" as a scare term, and is all the more challenging in *The Bell Curve* because it is backed by sub-stantial demographic data correlating intelligence and other social facts.[19]

The vigorous debate on measuring "heritability" is the latest form taken by the age-old conundrum on the role of nature versus nurture in creating personal and social differences. Improvement in the methods of quantifying both environmental and inherited influences will eventually make more precise *The Bell Curve*'s broad proposition that intelligence is substantially—in a range between 40 and 80 percent—derived from ge-netic sources. But even if the genetic factor were to be proven smaller and somewhat modifiable by education and social improvements, it would still make a competitive difference in an information economy, where intelligence is at perhaps a greater premium in day-to-day oper-ations than ever before. Where control functions are increasingly cen-tralized and therefore reduced in staffing, those with even a small differential in intelligence will tend to be selected for positions of re-sponsibility and hence prominence.

The threat of social domination by a controlling group of brainy tech-nologists, long the favored theme of futuristic novels and films, has gone beyond the political challenge of Young's *Meritocracy*, which envisions a welfare state run by civil servants in the mold of Labor intellectuals (the equivalent of New Deal brain-trusters). Beginning as a form of left-wing anxiety about a new source of inequality arising from programs to re-duce inequality, the angst then passed to right-wing pundits, who generalized from the sixties disturbance of social order and from radical posturing on the campuses to a perception of general leftward movement among a new class. Since then, alarms about the influence of the "cog-nitive elite" in Democratic circles have been sounded in Republican polemics, leading a keen observer to conclude, "The voguish idea that America is run by a small group of brainy people is a wild exaggeration, but it has its political uses."[20] Although overestimations of the New Class's current political influence can be corrected almost as readily as fears of its leftist orientation, the debate has called attention to an undoubted change in the balance of social forces. The presence of the college educated in substantial numbers—23 million with bachelor's degrees in the mid-nineties—and their conditioning by socially conscious, if only rarely radical, teachers and professors has made the more intelligent and better-educated a significant constituency in the body politic. And as the gap between those selected for and those remaining outside the information economy widens, the natural and nurtured differences between those with higher and those with lesser intelligence and education become more pronounced elements of their political and cultural behavior.

* * *

"Most readers of this book—this may be said because we know a great deal about the statistical tendencies of people who read a book like this—are in preposterously unlikely groups, and this reflects the degree of partitioning that has already occurred. . . . They constituted the thinnest cream floating on the surface of American society in 1930. In 1990, they constituted a class." *The Bell Curve* is probably unique among recent general interest publications in making explicit (here, on p. 47) its appeal to a sharply limited audience: "people who read a book like this." Were it not for its lack of euphony, such a phrase might serve for the group designated by Herrnstein and Murray as the "cognitive elite," and for a substantial portion of the New Class itself.

A number of points in their account are worth emphasizing. First, this is a historically emergent grouping, attaining critical mass from the change in educational recruiting traced in the book's first chapter: from college enrollment based on inherited status to test-based admissions policies that enabled highly endowed youth from all classes to attain college and postgraduate degrees. In consequence, while the college educated changed as a group from 1930 to 1990 not only in quantity but in class origins, higher education itself showed remarkable changes in student quality: "The largest change . . . has been the huge increase in the intelligence of the average student in the top dozen universities, up a standard deviation and a half from where the Ivies and the Seven Sisters were in 1930" (p. 46). Other institutions besides the elite schools have changed in this way, of course, but what is emphasized here is a transformation in their potential social effects: the products of selective and advanced education, who tend to achieve leadership positions, are more likely than before to be people of high intelligence—among graduates of the top dozen schools, 2.7 standard deviations above the general population mean.[21]

Further, "people who read a book like this" constitute a highly restricted group, even though greatly enlarged beyond the "thinnest cream" of the thirties. Although almost 10 percent of the national population sports a bachelor's degree, the audience for intellectually challenging studies of this kind is considerably smaller. To pursue the debatable but stimulating mental exercise proposed by the authors: "Think of your twelve closest friends or colleagues. . . . Many of you will not think it odd that half or more of the dozen have advanced degrees. But the odds against finding such a result among a randomly chosen group of twelve Americans are actually more than a million to one" (p. 47). The exercise, although far from a call to class self-consciousness, serves to underscore the cognitive elite's extreme selectness, despite its marked growth. People of this ilk are likely to bear their fate with mixed pride and embarrassment; in populist America, as Michael Lind reminds us, the "just folks" style is prevalent, designed to ward off not only imputations of snobbishness but any guilt harbored by those well favored by inheritance—in this case, genetic.

New Class members' conscientious response to their extraordinary luck and success has become visible in their increasing philanthropic activity. The multibillion-dollar Gates Foundation has, since his marriage, been promoting education and health efforts not only in the United States but globally; software billionnaire Peter Norton and his wife have invested in artworks by minority producers; mere millionnaires have addressed the environment, the advancement of women, and other worthy causes. A telling indication of these contributors' mentality comes from a participant in the founding of Amazon.com: "To figure out how to sell books on the Internet may be a hard problem. But to figure out what you want to change about the world and how to change that in an effective way that makes people better off, it's just a far vaster problem."[22] How well these philanthropic investments will work to deflect inevitable resentment in other classes—not to speak of leftist hostility toward a new oligarchy—remains to be seen, but may well follow the course of the capitalist conversion of, for example, the Rockefeller name from "robber baron" to endower of great public institutions.[23]

Remarkably, Herrnstein and Murray are explicit in describing this highly restricted group as a class. One of the channels by which the class character of a new group manifests itself lies in the way its formation affects other classes. On the family level, "the social fabric in the middle class and working class is altered when the most talented children of those families are so efficiently extracted to live in other worlds" (p. 49). As the authors continue, their description comes to resemble the account of a distinct class: "It is difficult to exaggerate how different the elite college population is from the population at large—first in its level of intellectual talent, and correlatively in its outlook on society, politics, ethics, religion, and all the other domains in which intellectuals, especially intellectuals concentrated into communities, tend to develop their own conventional wisdoms" (p. 50). *The Bell Curve* may be faulted for using a term, "intellectuals," with a far narrower reference than the more pertinent category, "readers of this book." The latter corresponds more closely with what we have been calling the New Class, of which, to be sure, many intellectuals are members. When the book became a *cause célèbre* for its focus on intelligence as a primary social force in contemporary life, many an intellectual became attentive, of course, but it was the broader audience of the New Class, aware that its own character and behavior were at issue, that made it, for a book of this technical complexity, something of a best-seller. No better single piece of evidence for the rising self-awareness of this class may be available than this publishing event. *The Bell Curve* may well have attracted the attention and, indeed, the opprobrium that it received because it speaks about and in some degree for the New Class.

* * *

In aligning Herrnstein and Murray's "readers of books like this" with the New Class, while learning to accept the apparently difficult truth of their superior intellectual talent, one must be cautious of the claimed differences between their attitudes and those of the general population. As established by many surveys (by Steven Brint and others), highly educated people's opinions on political and economic matters barely differ from other groups', although their social and educational emphases are distinctive. Only the degree of their political participation varies considerably from that of the population at large. *The Bell Curve* helps us to refine the common knowledge that voting is more common among the higher classes than among the lower: "the standard theory of political involvement for many years has assumed that socioeconomic status is the vital link. People at higher-status levels vote more, and they know and care more about political matters than do people at lower levels of status. But the available research offers ample evidence that the key element for predicting political involvement is educational level" (p. 253; italics omitted). In line with their emphasis on the social importance of cognitive ability, the authors go on to correlate educational with intelligence differences, so that greater political participation is associated with these key characteristics of the New Class. We've heard much journalese about "soccer moms," liberal on social issues, who've become the target of pollsters and partisans; a broader view would recognize the larger class to which many of these women, suburbanite and/or professional, belong. Such a view encourages us to believe that this gender contingent represents a class with greater-than-average commitment to social and educational improvement.

In the realm of religion, as in politics, there is evidence of class-based differences between the cognitive elite and the general public. A study cited in *The New York Times Magazine* (Dec. 7, 1997) found that although 87 percent of Americans expressed a belief in the resurrection of Jesus, "God does less well in cyberspace. One survey found that only 40 percent of on-line users consider themselves Christians, and just 65 percent believe in a supreme being. And 11 percent call themselves atheists (compared with 3 percent in the American population)." Tending in the same direction are data on ethical stances from the *New Yorker* survey (Jan. 5, 1998) cited in a previous chapter. When inspecting a population group of "college graduates aged between thirty and sixty whose personal (not family) income is more than a hundred thousand dollars a year,"[24] the survey found that almost nine of ten respondents in this group answered affirmatively when asked, "Do you believe in God?" but it also found that a significant portion defined God differently from the general population. Whereas the latter showed a higher preference for the personal god of theism, the select group showed a higher preference for the impersonal "force that created the universe and its laws, but does not intervene in the working of that creation." A rationalistic religious orientation, reminiscent of eighteenth-century deism, could be readily predicted of a social grouping formed on the basis of strong educational background and computerized workaday performance.

Finally, in the ethical sphere, generalizations about the cognitive elite are hard to come by. *The Bell Curve's* use of data on a so-called Middle Class Values Index is introduced almost apologetically, whereas *The New Yorker's* survey includes a report on a sample of its own subscribers— labeled without apology as the "cultural elite"—that indicates more tolerant attitudes toward gender deviance, marital infidelity, and the like than those of the general population. Insofar as the "cultural elite," defined and approached on a more solid basis than in this survey, may constitute a portion of the New Class, such evidence would be relevant. But it has yet to be established that this class, better informed than others about the world both past and present, has taken on the hedonism and ethical indifference ascribed to it by both liberal and conservative critics.[25]

None of the traits explored here is an exclusive characteristic of the New Class. Computerized relaxation, electronic socializing, an eroticized relation to technology, modern or postmodern loneliness and alienation, digitalized escapism, and even technobabble can make their appearance in many a specimen lacking one or more socioeconomic indicators of this class. Individuals with high intelligence (as the authors of *The Bell Curve* are careful to point out) are distributed throughout the class structure, although in varying degrees of incidence. A rationalistic trend in religious belief has been observable in many quarters, along with more glaring displays of irrationalism, and a broad shift toward greater ethical tolerance and guilt-free self-gratification, not confined to a specific group, has been the subject of numerous jeremiads. Yet the complex of socioeconomic attributes, social and personal attitudes, and patterns of behavior in work and play described above cannot be dismissed as merely human nature in its turn-of-the-millennium form. There is at least as much evidence here of a specific class personality type as has been employed to designate aristocrats, bourgeoisie, or proletarians in previous eras. The New Class may not be as enlightened and magnanimous as its promoters—or as radical and self-serving as its detractors—would have it, but by virtue of its capacity to deploy high intelligence in the social and cultural, perhaps even in the economic and political spheres, it may be, as Alvin Gouldner said of it, "the best card history has given us to play."

NOTES

1. James R. Beniger, *The Control Revolution: Technological and Economic Origins of the Information Society* (Cambridge, Mass., 1986).

2. The statistics are assembled in Stephen Moore and Julian L. Simon, *It's Getting Better All the Time: 100 Greatest Trends of the Last 100 Years* (Washington, D.C., 2000) and speak for themselves without the authors' tendentious asides.

3. A *New York Times Magazine* article (Oct. 10, 1999) on a leading industry figure—Jim Clark, a Stanford computer instructor who went on to found Silicon Graphics, Netscape, and Healtheon—raises the question of his proper occupational category: scientist, inventor, entrepreneur, and other terms for the stages of his activity are found inadequate.

4. The management efficiency guru Peter Drucker claims to have coined the term in *Landmarks of Tomorrow* (1959). It is prominent in former Labor Secretary Robert Reich's writings and speeches. Other terminology has become subject to ideological debate: "information economy," but not "information society," is acceptable in left-leaning social thought, for example, William Leiss, "The Myth of the Information Society," in Ian Angus and Sut Jhally, eds., *Cultural Politics in Contemporary America* (New York and London, 1989), pp. 282–298.

5. Peter N. Stearns, *American Cool: Constructing a Twentieth Century Emotional Style* (New York and London, 1994).

6. "Postmodernism, or The Cultural Logic of Late Capitalism," *New Left Review* 146 (1984), p. 83; the quotation that follows is from p. 92. This famous essay gives its title to a collection of Jameson's writings (Durham, N.C., 1991). Cf. David Harvey, *The Condition of Postmodernity: An Enquiry into the Origins of Cultural Change* (Oxford and Cambridge, Mass., 1989), which adds temporal disorientation to Jameson's spatial dislocation. Jameson holds out hopes, however,

for a "new political art," an undoubtedly radical "political form of postmodernism."

7. Francis Fukuyama, *The Great Disruption: Human Nature and the Reconstitution of Social Order* (New York, 1999). The degeneration statistics cited here, comparable to those assembled in such conservative barrages as William J. Bennett's *Index of Leading Cultural Indicators: American Society at the End of the Twentieth Century* (New York and Colorado Springs, Colo., 1999 [1994]), are challenged in Moore and Simon, *op. cit.*, p. 207 ff. as failing to reflect the turnaround in some of these parameters in the nineties. Bennett's introduction to the updated edition of his book acknowledges the improvements but deplores the remaining derelictions; Fukuyama seizes on similar evidence to hold out hope that the race's instinct for self-preservation will impose a new order.

8. Alvin and Heidi Toffler, *Creating a New Civilization: The Politics of the Third Wave* (Atlanta, 1994); foreword by Newt Gingrich.

9. Quoted in Michael Heim, *The Metaphysics of Virtual Reality* (New York and Oxford, 1993), p. 78.

10. Howard Rheingold, *The Virtual Community: Homesteading on the Electronic Frontier*, (Reading, Mass., 1993).

11. Sherry Turkle, *Life on the Screen: Identity in the Age of the Internet* (New York, 1995).

12. For example, those collected in Steven G. Jones, ed., *Virtual Culture: Identity and Communication in Cybersociety* (London, 1997).

13. Baudrillard's travel book, *America*, trans. Chris Turner (London and New York, 1988 [1986]), projects these features onto the national geography. A less rhetorical commentator is Gregory J.E. Rawlins, who carefully assesses the computer's outputs as a balance of gains and losses: *Moths to the Flame: The Seductions of Computer Technology* (Cambridge, Mass., and London, 1996).

14. Mark Dery, *Escape Velocity: Cyberculture at the End of the Century* (New York, 1996).

15. John A. Barry, *Technobabble* (Cambridge, Mass., and London, 1991). The quotation that follows is from p. 5 (italics omitted).

16. As described in his *I.Q. in the Meritocracy* (Boston and Toronto, 1973).

17. The book was published, in an act of some heroism, by The Free Press (New York, London) in 1994. The politicized response to it is, no doubt, partly motivated by its closing argument on the limited efficacy of affirmative action and other liberal policies, but only in response to that section is a discourse shift from psychological and social science to politics intellectually justified.

18. Michael Young, *The Rise of the Meritocracy: 1870–2033: An Essay on Education and Equality* (Baltimore, 1961 [1958]).

19. Herrnstein and Murray's data on the racial gap, its sources and interpretation, have been the object of self-confessed ideological critique by scholarly as well as lay opponents; the most systematic of these denigrations is *Inequality by Design: Cracking The Bell Curve Myth* (Princeton, N.J., 1996), by a team of mainly Berkeleyan social scientists (Claude S. Fischer's is the first name on the title page). An even more vigorous rebuttal is Robert L. Hayman, Jr., *The Smart Culture: Society, Intelligence, and Law* (New York and London, 1996), a product of the "critical legal studies" approach, which seems to take the position that *The Bell Curve*'s argument is racist even if true. The bottom line on these extended tirades

is drawn by a measured combatant, Glenn C. Loury: "Nobody disputes that people with better mental skills will, on average, perform better in our society. And, yes, this view is rather more broadly accepted now than it had been before the appearance of *The Bell Curve*. But Murray hasn't managed to answer the academic community's chief complaint: His theory does not adequately account for the role social environment plays in determining one's lot in life" ("Charles II: The Hard Questions," *The New Republic* [May 18, 1998], p. 10). Economists such as Loury have exhibited a degree of scientific detachment not always maintained in these discussions, for example, by proceeding with the cooperation of the surviving coauthor himself; see Kenneth Arrow, Samuel Bowles and Steven Durlauf, eds., *Meritocracy and Economic Inequality* (Princeton, N.J., 2000). Only one of these essays indulges in the favorite canard of guilt by association with the history of racist social science. A consensus emerges disputing *The Bell Curve*'s emphasis on intelligence's economic and social effects without considering the concomitant efficacy of education, thus holding out hope for reducing inequality through educational improvement. This is of course a traditional progressive approach, but in the current state of the American educational system it seems to offer only guarded expectations.

20. Nicholas Lemann, "A Cartoon Elite," *Atlantic Monthly* (Nov. 1996), p. 109. Lemann's *The Big Test: The Secret History of the American Meritocracy* (New York, 1999), on the Educational Testing Service and the unfairness of using its Scholastic Aptitude Test to select college material on the basis of "innate ability," suffers from the populist anxieties he elsewhere decries. Its conclusion that a fairer selection could be based on students' mastery of a national secondary-school curriculum is salutary in calling attention to the inequities and incoherence of our localized educational diversity, but it avoids reckoning with the alternative meritocracy that would inevitably be formed.

21. For those, like myself, not easily conversant with such expressions, the authors add a free translation: "as a measure of distance from the mean, one standard deviation means 'big,' two standard deviations means 'very big,' and three standard deviations means 'huge' " (p. 44).

22. Quoted in *The New York Times*, Feb. 11, 2000.

23. An assortment of liberal responses to the growing income inequality is discussed in Mickey Kaus, *The End of Equality* (New York, 1992), p. 32 ff., which also takes up the intelligence factor in determining income growth and consequent inequality.

24. Hendrik Hertzberg, reporting this survey, labels this segment the "economic elite," reserving the category "cultural elite" for another population group, subscribers to *The New Yorker*.

25. A particularly egregious example is Dana Mack, *The Assault on Parenthood: How Our Culture Undermines the Family* (New York, 1997), which posits that progressive educators are leading the New Class in a campaign to revise the middle-class value system.

5

New Class/New Culture

"You've arrived!"
—the Thin Man to Mrs. Charles, at a wrestling match

Just as, in every society beyond the tribal level, one or another class has tended to dominate, a single art, or style, or genre has been the dominant cultural form. Marxist notions of culture's derivation from an economic "base" need not be invoked to ground these observations, for it was a leading theoretician among the Russian formalists, Roman Jakobson, who orginated this concept of the cultural dominant. The idea gains confirmation when one recalls the cultural periods and places when, for example, Romantic poetry or Victorian fiction were the leading arts of their time. The music of the Romantic period and the poetry of the Victorian are not thereby slighted: rather, the inspirational energy of the dominant style or genre carries the sister arts to higher achievements than they might otherwise have attained. When assessing the current state of American culture, it would be useful to widen the view beyond local trends and reflect on the peculiar fact that two distinct phenomena emerged at about the same time: postmodernism in culture and the New Class in society. Is it conceivable that these two developments, each of them amply grounded in the history of art and society, nonetheless have some deeper relationship, homology (to use a term favored by neo-Marxist sociologists of culture), or affiliation?

Neither the New Class nor postmodernism are unequivocally dominant in their respective realms. Yet both are notable for adding a novel element to the social and cultural fields, an element that changes all relations among the prior constituents. Other classes, other styles remain active and important, while the recent entrants introduce a keen stimulus toward a reconfigured structuring of the social or cultural whole. American society still has its traditional social strata yet has never before been what it is today, given the presence of the New Class. Similarly, American culture has its spheres of traditional, mass-produced, and modernist cultures yet will never be the same after the advent of postmodernism. Without designating postmodernism as the culture of the New Class, it is plausible that the invigorating influence of these recent entrants in their respective spheres is derived from their underlying affinities.

A name for a key component in the complex of attitudes that are exhibited both in the everyday behavior of the New Class and in the circulation of postmodern arts is "knowingness." Several alternative terms have been employed, each with shortcomings in precisely capturing this quality or in its range of application. An obvious synonym is "sophistication," but its overtones of worldly experience don't securely apply to recent recruits to the New Class, although their growing acquaintance with the world through the Web gives promise of eventual cosmopolitan attitudes, a subject to be explored in the next chapter. The more frequently employed term for the postmodern stance is "skepticism," and considerable philosophic powers have been deployed either to advance skeptical approaches to art and other experiences or to deplore the trend in this direction.[1] Although abundant skepticism is present in the operational logic of both New Class professionals and postmodern artists—in their acceptance of provisional arrangements for workable solutions, rather than strict adherence to abstract principle or tradition—the systematic negativism usually associated with the term renders it something of a red herring, since such negativism isn't highly visible among the New Class and is rampant only among the more ideological artists and critics.

Another often heard term, "irony," has strong claims to be applied to postmodern art and lesser but still plausible ones to refer to New Class attitudes, yet the word is most useful when taken together with an accompanying polar term, "nostalgia"—the former signaling cool detachment from the past and its products, and the latter a lingering desire for things lost or lacking.[2] An even stronger form of distancing, cynicism, has also been polemically ascribed to both camps, but it overestimates the element of levity or parody and gratuitously impugns the seriousness of both the class and the art in question. "Self-consciousness" is surely a useful way of describing their heightened awareness of past forms of art and behavior and their willingness to modify these in experimental or provisional ways, yet the depth of this awareness remains uncertain.

Self-consciousness brings into play a category that has traditionally been called "selfhood," and it is unclear to what extent either the New Class or postmodernism remains devoted to its enrichment.[3] Both pronouncements of antisubjectivity (for example, the poststructuralist rejection of the "bourgeois subject") and traditionalist laments over diminished awareness of the self have arisen with postmodern art, yet subjectivity remains visible enough. "Selfishness" or its variants has, of course, been liberally attributed to both this class and this art, but these pejoratives refer to behaviors independent of and perhaps coexistent with deeper self-consciousness.

Given these limitations in the alternative terms for the common factor in New Class and postmodern thinking and performance, I take "knowingness" to be a nontendentious and appropriate label for this slippery phenomenon. The abruptness of the entry of both these forces on the contemporary scene leads to a hypothesis on the psychic sources of this, their common factor. Knowingness may well be a compensatory stance, given the anxieties of novelty: people who are not necessarily insecure in their position but unable to feel confident of the reasons for performing as they do are likely to acquaint themselves with the alternatives, both past and present, so as to underwrite their activities as preferable, given the other options. Knowingness becomes not merely a device for covering oneself where critical and operational norms are shaky or absent, but a pathway toward a wider comprehension of the activity one's engaged in, whether it be computerized problem-solving or artistic innovation. One might also adduce the palpable anxiety generated by the dizzying rate of innovation and obsolescence in computer-related fields— not to speak of the stock market, which is so closely tied to them—and by the rapid succession of cutting-edge styles in the postmodern arts. Anxiety is never pleasant but it is well known as a potent and potentially useful psychological stimulus. I propose in what follows that the knowingness that accompanies anxieties of this kind holds the promise of generating a valuable state of mind in both cultural creators and cultural recipients. This state of mind, the esthetic attitude, has a long pedigree and shows some recent setbacks, but its sustenance may become an unintended outcome of the forces shaping New Class behavior and postmodern art.

* * *

One need not look far to find manifestations of knowingness in the arts and media. In television, the comedic style of David Letterman represents an extreme instance of a trend toward undercutting one's own and others' self-presentations, with accompanying smirks for conventions and predecessors. Theatrical performances that mock the texts they enact, especially by pointed use of contemporary sets and costumes, have reached an apogee or nadir in the opera stagings of Peter Sellars. So diffused has this tendency become that television critics such as Mark Crispin Miller have deplored the cynicism that seems its underlying attitude.[4] Yet an audience aware of tradition and convention, on which such undercuttings depend, can also be relied on to recognize and accept the rising use of visual techniques and plot and character twists hitherto restricted to avant-garde theater, fiction, and cinema. Giving greater substance to Marshall MacLuhan's notion that the "medium is the message" than it had previously attained, the use of voice-over, split screen, and color/black-and-white contrasts to convey subjective experience (for example, in the *Ally McBeal* and *Once and Again* series) has come to television in ways that call unprecedented attention to the means of presentation. Knowingness in performance media shows itself capable both of fostering mindless reduction to the absurd and expanding drama's expressive range through enhanced audiovisual techniques.

In cinema, especially, the fortunes of knowingness have been mixed. On the one hand, the popularity of recycled successes—all those *Aliens* and *Halloweens* and *Screams*—has reinforced the Hollywood-to-Hong-Kong imperative to do again what has profitably been done before. Some of these series have made the audience's knowingness an explicit feature by alluding not merely to prior events in the story but to earlier films in the sequence. (*Scream III* even dramatizes the shooting of prior events as a film within the film, in what literary theorists call *mise en abîme* construction.) Although the Hollywood industry's preference for the kinetic—movement on the screen and in the audience members' viscera— has furthered its current creative doldrums, a countertrend toward using avant-garde techniques in mainstream products is also notable. Films such as *Pleasantville* and *The Truman Show* employ a wide range of technical devices for presenting distinct narrative worlds: a contemporary frame story plus past television's never-never land in the former case, a realm of manipulators plus a manipulated hero in an artificial town in the latter. New ground in the creation of surreal worlds is also being broken in the films of David Lynch and in the even more hypothetical realm of *Being John Malkovich* (whose compexity did not block it from winning a number of Academy Awards). Radical experimentalism that exploits the audience's awareness of the medium and its history carries no guarantee of artistic success, as the record of both modernism and postmodernism bears out, yet it is a sign of life in an art form that has otherwise come far from the days of Griffith and Welles, of Bergman and Fellini.

In literature, a similar set of mixed blessings may be accounted to the growing willingness of readers to remain aware that fictional worlds are produced by artful and conventional means, which are often as interesting in themselves as the reality effects they produce. This widespread acceptance of or indulgence in the fictionality of fiction depends at least in part on the expansion of a college-educated readership, one that has been alerted by savvy teachers to the self-referential traits and multiple "reality" realms of novels from *Don Quixote* and *Tristram Shandy* down through *Ulysses* and *Gravity's Rainbow*. It is this substantial audience, overlapping though not identical to the New Class, that makes possible the relatively high popularity of authors such as Thomas Pynchon and John Barth, who would otherwise have shared the fate—honored but neglected—of John Hawkes and William Gaddis. So prominent has fiction in this vein become—one thinks of Paul Auster, Robert Coover, David Foster Wallace et al.—that one rising author has mildly protested: "Writers my age ... don't have the luxury of a choice. Our problem is how to confront the influence of a single novelist: Thomas Pynchon."[5] However much individuals may personalize the trend, making Pynchon the one to emulate if not to beat at his own game, the larger point is clear: contemporary fiction aspiring to goals other than the best-seller lists or the shelf space devoted to the romances is squarely based on theoretical premises articulated by obscure postmodern theorists yet casually accepted by a substantial reading public.[6]

The cultural realm in which the New Class, especially when engaged in home building and furnishing, is most visibly activated by postmodern impulses is that of architecture and product design.[7] Class-identifying and self-expressive impulses, reciprocal inclinations toward irony and nostalgia, are given ample scope here in the anxiety-tinged effort to find a solid base in tradition, while making the requisite moves toward demonstrating knowing detachment and inventive novelty. Now that the shock effect of the revivalist 1980s architecture has run its course, one can look on it as acting out a deeper tendency in postmodernism, the intellectual trait that goes by the neologism, "recuperation." The word is used in theoretical discourse, in its French not its English sense, to refer not to the mind's or body's efforts to restore itself after trauma, but to intellectual moves designed to recover for a term or concept the elements it has excluded. Hence its frequent negative connotation, suggesting that in choosing A over B, but then recuperating B in subsequent provisos, thinker X has sold out to B and its patrons after all. More persuasively, the dual impulse in postmodern architecture—and the double motivation of many a New Class participant in renovation activities—is to have it both ways: to catch a ray from the past's aura while placing oneself at the cutting edge in technological means or imaginative outcomes.

In the New Class's domestic arrangements, recuperation signals less a reverent attitude toward the past and its treasures—whether a derelict building up for clearance or a patinated painting on an auction platform—than a desire for repossession (to adopt the language of real estate financing). This is no merely acquisitive motive: a reader, viewer, or auditor taking possession of an esthetic object may be affected as profoundly as one is in being possessed of a personal attribute, and for an artist to be possessed by a vision and the urge to realize it may be more admirable still. New Class possessiveness takes steps beyond merely collecting and savoring objects and experiences, in the direction of recontextualizing, adapting the object to its own needs, terms, or self-conceptions. Contextual recodings are endemic in all cultural activity, of course, and all traditions continually modify their sources. Yet New Class recuperation declares its lacks and desires both more assertively and more pathetically than most others. These are people who appear hungry for cultural content; both they and their experts—architects, designers, decorators, craftsmen, and so on—have become skilled in filling genuine needs. Nor is the professional game plan mere catering to an upscale market, devoid of reverence for traditional materials and images. Testimony to the sincere historicism of at least some postmodern architects—not always clearly readable from their buildings—is convincingly offered by Robert A.M. Stern: "The story I seek to tell is that of America, or more precisely what it means to be an American."[8]

Recuperation implies a conjuncture of past and present: mixing of media, styles, and genres is inherent in such processes. Configurations of the ethnically distinctive and the abstractly universal, like the homely homes of Frank Gehry or Robert Venturi; recoveries of the archaic, such as cast-iron loft buildings installed with high-tech appurtenances and equipment; home-furnishing plans and provisions that mingle the quaint and the glitzy—these are not to be put down as mere kitsch but are consistent with a distinct style, which I've called the culture of blurring. In the perspective of historical periodization—if we may anticipate a long-range view of the present—today's domestic and institutional style is the expression of a genuine social phenomenon and hence a valid and authentic entrant on the cultural scene. Its *arriviste* modishness is compensated for by its evident virtues: a curiosity, sometimes rising to enthusiasm, about the full range of cultural goods; an abundant investment of intelligence, bolstered by considerable educational attainments; a refreshing freedom to select and reject according to felt sympathies rather than inherited prejudices.

The downside—there's always a downside—is the transitory and provisional character of the works generated and the appreciation devoted to them. Both Mies van der Rohe's Seagram Building and Philip Johnson's AT&T (now Sony) Building remain imposing marks on the New York townscape, but the one speaks of the twentieth century and the other of a brief spate of fashion within it. One need not join the architectual clan currently promoting a return of classical proportions and ornament to affirm that traditional, including modern, forms can be sources of stability rather than imported decoration, merely cosmetic and soon passé. Recent designs aspire to capture qualities that promise endurance if not permanence: who can doubt that the whiteness of Richard Meier's buildings are reminiscences of classicism—his Los Angeles hilltop Getty Center suggesting a new Acropolis—with dreams of a like longevity?[9] How well these structures prevail in the long term is less significant, perhaps, than their provision for the sources of both irony and nostalgia.

Although postmodern architecture has recovered from its high-jinks phase—Gehry moving beyond his binocular shaped office building in Venice, California, to his space-age museum form in Bilbao, Spain—all is not well in other arts, where changing and mixing of styles has led away from permanence or even the dream of permanence.[10] Contemporary composition that aspires to the status of classical music has largely passed beyond esoteric serialism and mystical minimalism, without discovering a successor style to stimulate even the temporary popularity of these stages, but the transitoriness of postmodern culture is nowhere more evident than in the visual arts. A scan of Irving Sandler's multiple volumes on postwar, primarily American, movements reveals a kaleidoscope of stylistic change like none other in the history of art. For the postmodern phase alone, Sandler covers the following: postminimalism, pattern and decoration painting, new image painting, neoexpressionism, media art, deconstruction art, commodity art, neogeo . . . the list goes on.[11] This kaleidoscope turns without obliterating the participants, instead repositioning them in successive configurations in which each remains visible, if only as a wan reminder of enthusiasms past. Nothing is lost from the intensive activity of these decades; nothing retains its initial singularity, either, which comes to be recognized as a move or position in the art field's structure.

* * *

Another recognition that stems from rising and falling style preferences is that they often track the pattern of rise and fall in the art market, which is itself conditioned by the stock and other markets. (The causal relations in this conjuncture have yet to be worked out; what is observable is the close association of stylistic tastes and market conditions.) There's nothing new about commercial pressures in art history, of course, but their entry into esthetic projects such as museum shows—where corporate sponsorship of exhibits featuring corporate products or collections is standard practice—suggests that little can be said or done in this field without counting the financial interests.[12] These interests are well recognized and generally deplored, even by artists who handsomely profit by them, but cannot be avoided, for they reflect socioeconomic realities. The wealthy have long dominated the art market; the New Class's entry into the field has helped to reshape it.

Although the blockbuster exhibits and record prices of impressionist and postimpressionist paintings (and for a few contemporaries) have focused attention on the high rollers in the market, the wide distribution of lesser commodities, products of the more than a million artists at work in this country, points to a broader range of consumers affluent enough for the spiritual exercise of art collecting.[13] According to expert estimates, there were by the end of the eighties "400,000 serious collectors world-wide—'serious' meaning that they spent at least $10,000 a year in the art market," compared with "between 250 and 350 *very* serious collectors, whose collections are worth millions." Many of these neophyte art patrons are recent entrants into the higher financial categories, and among them stands a portion of the New Class.

The inaugural date for the postwar art field's crystallization—often put at 1959, when Robert Rauschenberg introduced Jasper Johns to his dealer, Leo Castelli—could at least as effectively be placed in 1972, when a number of uptown New York dealers opened SoHo galleries and began selling contemporary prints as well as paintings. All that followed seems in retrospect to have been necessary and appropriate: a growing body of collectors with new money and relatively unformed taste, a turn in esthetic theory and critical practice away from the modernist norms that guided previous twentieth-century art, and a freshly tailored corps of producers, spawned by the art schools' equivalent of the postwar explosion in higher education enrollment. It would be a surrender to economic determinism to conclude that the advent of new-moneyed collectors *made* the market, the artists, and the art itself, but their presence in the pattern must be considered as striking an instance of class culture—of emergent classes stimulating high activity and appropriate styles—as the turn-of-the-century Gilded Age art, spawned by capitalism's heyday.

The representative status of Andy Warhol and his works in this later gilded age was recognized by many, including the maker himself, in his frank acknowledgment of art as commerce. The often quoted remark by a fellow artist that "Warhol was the perfect glass and mirror of his age and certainly the artist we deserved" paints this iconic figure with his own favored mixture of irony and naïveté.[14] The shape of his career, rapidly ascendant, tragically terminated, with an afterlife descending to crime and farce in the saga of his foundation and executors, is a postmodern version of the romantic artist as *poète maudit*. But not all accursed artists die in a garret. The estimated half-billion-dollar value of Warhol's estate is an indicator of the vast financial investment and ultimately of class influence in the shaping of postmodern art.[15]

Yet the power of big money to magnify limited talents such as Warhol's could not by itself have generated the wide dissemination and warm public response to his works that made them cultural icons. "More people visited the Warhol retrospective [in 1989 at New York's Museum of Modern Art] than those visiting the major exhibitions at MoMA of Picasso, Braque or Matisse," it was reported. His presence in the major museums, the awed attention accorded to his often clumsy or deliberately banal reproductions of commercial labels, ads, and media images, as well as of masterpieces such as *The Last Supper*, testify to the workings of forces beyond the simply financial that made him the representative artist of our time. (Not the jaded alone will mutter, *Quel artiste, quel temps.*)

The cast of mind that Warhol exercised finds expression in cultural fields beyond the visual arts. An insight into underlying connections in the pop music field is offered by a *New York Times* specialist who points out the similarities between his techniques of appropriating mercantile and other cultural symbols, from soup can labels to celebrity photos, and the pop methods of "sampling" selections from previous hits so as to generate nostalgic recollections or provide grist for creative reformulation.[16] The key to this linkage is the similar effect of the technologies employed in these very different media: in Warhol's (and subsequent imitators') case, enlarged and silk-screened photos are printed onto painted canvases; in the music industry, the digital instrument called a sampler, in the hands of the recording artist known as a remixer, modifies and arranges snippets of sound to produce new pieces. (One song in this, the "electronica" genre, claims to employ about three hundred samples.) "The challenge is not to fabricate something new," Tony Scherman notes, "but to cast the already fabricated in a new light." Or as Warhol put it, "The selection of the images is the most important [thing] and is the fruit of the imagination."

This pervasive move, not merely to appropriate but to refabricate the previously fabricated, expands the generative possibilities of "the work of art in the age of mechnical production" beyond Walter Benjamin's vision of copious replication in photography and cinema. Machine production favors repetition, and "seriality" becomes the most visible and audible impact of these trends in both media. Warhol's multiplication, on a single surface, of celebrity portraits or disaster scenes is by now familiar. Similarly, electronica and hip-hop string together one- and two-bar sound loops—in repetitive sequences. Nor is this foregrounding of basic units, the expansion of the elements into larger structures, confined to pop music: it is the favored mode of avant-garde composers such as Philip Glass and Steve Reich. By means of repetitive series (whose effects are quite different from the constant surprises of serialism), these and other "classical" composers go beyond the modernist impulse to rework jazz rhythms and folk themes. The appearance of these creative approaches in a number of media (similar traits are observable in literature and cinema) strongly suggests that appropriation-reformulation-repetition is the esthetic "dominant" of turn-of-the-millennium culture.

* * *

Who is served by this dominant? Or, to put the question in the form favored by the current argument: how is the New Class particularly, as well as others in varying degrees, served by it? The beginning of wisdom on these questions resides in coupling two remarks by a well-connected observer of recent trends. Louis Menand expresses the official line on postmodernism's trumping of modernism in these terms: "This liberation of art from abstract prior conceptions was one of the great achievements of American culture in the Sixties."[17] Menand locates this rejection of modernist norms not in the recherché skepticism of postmodernist theory but in a more pervasive change: an intellectually browbeaten "middlebrow" audience liberated by the likes of Pauline Kael, movie reviewer for *The New Yorker*, who made "popular entertainment respectable to people whose education told them that popular entertainment is not art" (p. 14). More persuasive than his simplistic formula that "Postmodernism in the arts simply is anti-essentialism" (p. 16) is Menand's phrase for the sociological event: "postmodernism was a middlebrow phenomenon" (p. 17). Although the sources of postmodern thinking must be sought in a broader intellectual history, this sketch of the process by which postmodern esthetic values were promulgated by critics indifferent if not hostile to theory and snapped up in a class culture bears the ring of truth.

Of which class are we speaking here? The once largely upper-middle class readers of *The New Yorker*, Menand implies, since these were Kael's immediate audience, but that segment is obviously too narrow to cover the audience for postmodernism, just as "middlebrow" is imprecise in referring to "people whose education told them that popular entertainment is not art." The answer, the New Class, only invites the further question, Why did this grouping, which partially overlaps the upper-middle class, suddenly find itself liberated by antitheoretical postmodern critics and welcome the pattern of appropriation-reformulation-repetition in various media?

As the course of Menand's argument, negotiating the thickets of the high-low controversy, makes clear, he is concerned about showing that popular culture (or elements of it) has been rightfully raised to an honorable place in educated taste. He and other proponents of a lightened-up mentality are certainly right about one thing: postmodern art is lighter than much of modernism (although one mustn't forget the wit of great modern painters and sculptors, nor that of Stravinsky or Auden).

It would be dogmatic to declare that the inherent value of much of this art amounts to kitsch, but a fair estimate of its social functioning would acknowledge that it performs the same social role as kitsch's. An art based on the dominant strategies of appropriation, reformulating new acquisitions with both irony and nostalgia, and rubbing it in with copious repetition, is clearly performing an educative function. In Abraham A. Moles's wise words on "the pedagogical function of kitsch," "In a bourgeois society, *and generally in a meritocratic one*, the passage through kitsch is the *normal passage* in order to reach the genuine. . . . Kitsch is pleasurable to the members of mass society, and through pleasure, it allows them to attain the level of higher exigencies and to pass from sentimentality to sensation. . . . Kitsch is essentially an aesthetic system of mass communication."[18] Whatever the degree of campy knowingness moving its creators to freewheeling manipulation, its social effect lies in orienting its recipients toward prior art, reorienting them toward cultural symbols, and providing a stance toward the objects of contemporary experience. The crowds of mainly youngish people gathered around the paintings of Jasper Johns at the Museum of Modern Art's 1996 exhibition were relearning how to look at the American flag—at the "ghost of the American flag," as one critic put it—just as their encounters with Warhol and Rauschenberg works teach cool responses to the *disjecta membra* of contemporary civilization huddled together there. Just as young television viewers report on surveys that they'll watch only shows about people like themselves, members of the well-educated audience, many of them of the New Class, want an art that responds to their commodious idea of the world they inhabit, a world felt but not grasped as an extension of themselves. "Narcissism" and "self-absorption" have been terms liberally strewn over the New Class and its culture; it should be accepted that learning how to look at oneself and one's world is an appropriate and potentially rewarding esthetic behavior.

The genius of postmodern artistry, when it succeeds, is to make this learning process something of a pleasure. The pleasure principle in esthetic experience has had a revival of late, with culture critics as temperamentally different as Camille Paglia and Wendy Steiner coming down strongly on the side of art as fun.[19] Much of this talk is framed within the discourse of cultural politics, as a response either to the heavy seriousness of "politically correct" art (Paglia) or to the anti-intellectual puritanism of conservative attacks on contemporary culture (Steiner). But it helps to explain the impulse in much postmodern art, pointed out by Menand, to allow the well educated to feel comfortable while rooting about in popular culture.[20] It should not be forgotten that creating as well as experiencing art has been said to be stimulating, even erotic, and it is evident that many a contemporary is passing along her enthusiasm, along with the product itself. In the period when a newly emergent class is guiding a technology that has, despite recessions, led the national economy to unprecedented wealth and nearly full employment, it is not to be wondered at that the predominant tone of art-making and art reception is on the whole upbeat. Jeff Koons's gigantic floral puppy dog (once displayed at Rockefeller Center and inevitably bound for the recycling bin) is merely its biggest toy.

* * *

Although many members of the New Class, despite layoffs and bankruptcies in computer and other fields, are doing very well financially, features of their cultural behavior have called critical attention to them, not all of it approving. Passing beyond the initial resentment that made "yuppie" a pejorative for a time, the more serious critique of this class's cultural style and influence targets its omissions rather than its preferences. One of the most glaring of these is the lack of any central or ordering principle by which its cultural choices might be made, its experiences and acquisitions graded. Some members attempt to overcome this state of ambiguity by testing the boundaries of permissible taste, in a vague echo of avant-garde extremism. A passage in Pierre Bourdieu's *Distinction*, although describing the New Class somewhat differently from the current account, nonetheless captures the note of anxiety as well as of assertiveness in its culture. Bourdieu's version of the New Class includes workers lacking in the advanced education emphasized above, focusing instead on their participation in "all the occupations involving presentation and representation . . . in all the institutions involving symbolic goods and services," that is, advertising, glossy journalism, fashion, and the like. His account of these symbol manipulators, irrespective of its peculiar national features, rings true of a broad pattern:

Their ambivalent relationship with the educational system, inducing a sense of complicity with every form of symbolic defiance, inclines them to welcome all the forms of culture which are, provisionally at least, on the (lower) boundaries of legitimate culture—jazz, cinema, strip cartoons, science fiction—and to flaunt (for example) American fashions and models—jazz, jeans, rock or the avant-garde underground, which is their monopoly—as a challenge to legitimate culture; but they often bring into these regions disdained by the educational establishment an erudite, even "academic" disposition which is inspired by a clear intention of rehabilitation, the cultural equivalent of the restoration strategies which define their occupational project.[21]

Just as the kitsch-oriented break from modernist norms was subsequently grounded in postmodernist theorizing, the self-liberating bottom fishing of symbol manipulators and analysts breeds an "erudite" disposition that seeks to justify their enthusiasms. Nor is it only mass-cultural art forms that seem to their devotees to require validation; the New Class's forays into traditional high culture (Bourdieu's "legitimate" culture) are marked by the same embarrassed need to solidify newly acquired tastes. For them, ventures into, say, original instrument performances of baroque music are as much in need of a rationale as those into zydeco or klezmer music and similarly call for learned contextual matter to ground them. These activities, benign and enlightening in themselves, betray anxiety surrounding the suspicion that there may be good reasons why Bach and Handel have had a longer and wider hold on music listeners than zydeco and klezmer bands.

A further aspect of New Class culture that exposes it to disdain may receive more sympathetic understanding through another implication of Bourdieu's remarks. The parallel he notes between the "rehabilitation" motives behind erudite justifications of "symbolic defiance" and the "restoration strategies" any New Class–favored vocations and avocations points to their convergence in daily living. Without denying either the social benefit of many restoration efforts or their practical advantages for those who've created attractive homes in the shells of inner-city buildings, it is evident that these activities carry a symbolic status value as well. Like the learned rationales for defiant leisure tastes—one thinks of serious consideration of rap lyrics as poetry—the gentrification of neighborhoods, houses, furniture, and so on marks the makers and owners as people of a special sort: the postmodern equivalent of gentry. Recycling of disused buildings for dwellings, shops, and ateliers, refurbishing or reproducing of old-fashioned clothing and artifacts, seems innocent, even worthy, but conveys a class-conscious message. With all its democratic sampling of the culture of all classes and ethnicities, despite its standard disavowal of class hierarchy in taste, the New Class announces itself as a class by its dressed-down and renovated-up accoutrements. And the social ascendance announced by many a demonstration of New Class culture is ironically underscored by the populist slogans that often accompany them.

From the postmodernist theoretical premises by now widely distributed in the educated public at large, an ethical as well as an esthetic orientation emerges: just as all cultural artifacts, including scholarly and scientific ones, are historically determined—"socially constructed," in the currently fashionable phrase—and thus equally valid as expressions of a social group, so all goals and values are merely personal or collective preferences and can have no lasting authority, lacking a foundation in or beyond human nature. Just as in pragmatist or utilitarian philosophy there are warranted calculations to justify truth claims or place limitations on hedonism, postmodernist thinkers have labored with varying conviction to find a warrant for ethical action and esthetic preferences.[22]

The fall into hedonism or nihilism that seems to follow from a mentality of this kind has been denounced not only by spokesmen of the right but by left-leaning moralists such as Christopher Lasch and Terry Eagleton.[23] Yet for all their determined participation in the consumer society, the well-educated members of the New Class have shown themselves perfectly capable of delaying immediate gratification on the grand scale in favor of long-term benefits for themselves and others, investing in and creating new enterprises, often with social-service functions. For all the talk of the new hedonism—amounting, when produced at the scale of an entire edition of *The New York Times Magazine* ("The Me Millennium," Oct. 17, 1999), to an arguable cliché—it does not notably exceed that of higher and lesser classes, and is certainly modest by comparison with that of previous rising classes in history.

Where the ethical and esthetic limitations on postmodernist thinking join together to produce a worrisome cultural deficiency is the realm of what used to be called higher values. An "object of loyalty" of a collective character would, given this mentality's presuppositions, be hard to come by.[24] This lacuna has usually been discussed as a loss of religious commitment but is of wider consequence, taking in the diminished aura of national symbols, artistic creators, and historical heroes. By the same logic, the dignity of art itself has come into question, not only by extremists devoted to undermining all traditional forms of dignity, but in the easygoing acceptance of art's provisions for entertainment, without reference to its long-assumed capacity for enlarging vision and ennobling creator and recipient alike. These values—those of the late-Enlightenment tradition of *Bildung* in education and of the Romantic "cult" (as it has been termed) of the artist as hero—have become inoperative in sophisticated cultural circles and obsolete in intellectual discourse. To measure the distance we've come, a thought experiment might be proposed: try to imagine a postmodern artist or critic writing an essay "on the spiritual in art," the title of a text by a founder of modern art.[25]

In the absence of collective objects of loyalty, a relatively recent entrant into the field of cultural discourse, feminism, has come forward to promote ethical and esthetic aspirations that go well beyond its initial aim at political and economic equality. Reviving the elevated rhetoric favored by the movement's nineteenth-century founders, recent feminist thinkers add a spiritual aura to the practical goals that have lost saliency since their substantial fulfillment. Celebrating the antiquity, unity, and super-rational wisdom of the sex itself or of their maternal forebears, they introduce into postmodern culture such arcana as the Great Mother goddess of ancient religions or the yet more remarkable Women Who Run with the Wolves. This disposition, although it sells a lot of books (see the Women's section in the bookstore chains), has yet to become widespread among the New Class, or even among the intelligentsia, though it is featured by a coterie of women artists and has attained academic standing in Women's Studies departments.[26] In the absence of widely shared collective values, people who need them, as many seem to do, will invent them or take to those offered by intellectuals and artists, whose social function is, in part, precisely this invention. We need not fear a New Class lapse into cultist behavior, though youthful dalliance with degeneracy has been noted on college campuses and in secondary schools. More troubling are the many indications that the deviant, the half-baked, and the irrational are becoming worthy esthetic goals and satisfactions.[27]

In a broader view of culture, one that encompasses the awareness of a nation's identity, postmodern challenges to received ideas, symbols, and heroes have had a steadily eroding effect. Not that symbols such as the Statue of Liberty or the avuncular Lincoln image have been discarded (though Jefferson's has been thoroughly trashed); they have been retained in the way other objects of past significance have been recycled in rehabbing practices. In the more advanced forms of the new thinking—which have not as yet been adopted by most members of the New Class—family, nation, and humanity are ruled out as authorizing concepts to guide individual choice and action. (Their revival in the present time of troubles has come without intellectual sanction.) Academic revisions of the schools' history curriculum are scenes of contention; museum exhibits of historical experiences from the settlement of the West to the dropping of the atomic bomb become *causes célèbres*; the idea and elements of a national standard of cultural knowledge are derided by leading postmodernist theoreticians. Undermining the long-standing assumptions of a nation founded in the Enlightenment, the idea of an essential human nature and the universal political rights that flow from it have been relegated to the dustbin of rationalizing mystifications. Although antihumanist relativists are no doubt troubled by the horrors of Rwanda and Kosovo, there is no movement of artists and intellectuals in support of efforts to bring mass criminals to justice, only an attitudinizing indulgence in rerunning the woes of the Holocaust. There are, however, signs of unease among postmodern intellectuals about completely abandoning the idea of universal human rights, when it comes to protecting at least selected victims of state oppression.[28] And as the next chapter will attempt to assess, there are indications that the New Class bears the potential if not for revolutionary liberation, as previous observers hoped or feared, at least for a more thoughtful and better-informed view of humanity than might have been expected from so affluent and self-gratifying a social group.

* * *

As its name suggests, postmodern culture is temporally rather than essentially defined. Although several striking tendencies of this culture's creators and participants have been noted here and elsewhere, it is above all its systematic changefulness that marks its art as historically unique. Even the postmodern architectural style that seemed distinctive for a decade or so has run its course, with no clear successor at the crest of the next wave. Predictions of cultural trends are likely to resemble those in the fashion industry rather than those of politics or economics (and even these are suspect), yet it is worth wondering aloud about where we go from here.

Perhaps surprisingly, it is a social scientist rather than a culture critic who most plausibly anticipates coming cultural patterns. Jeffrey C. Alexander, in *Fin de Siècle Social Theory*,[29] provides a useful charting of successive developments in the history of modernism, thereby enabling a prospect of its future course, broadly sketched though that must be. A sociopolitical perspective makes clear that postmodernism didn't arise out of the intellectual or esthetic program of one or another clique—whether the antirationalist Continental deconstructionists or the populist promulgators of the low along with the high in American culture—but was a more pervasive shift, an international reordering of attitudes and behavior in line with the emergence of a new social class. It also adds depth to the casual observation that all this began with or in the "sixties," a word that has acquired a resonance usually reserved for terms such as "the revolution" or "the millennium." I follow Alexander's rubrics in summarizing these transitions.

Although *modernism* was as complex a cultural movement as any in the history of art and ideas; although its political relationships were so tangled as to range from fascism (Ezra Pound) to communism (numerous fellow travelers), and from Lionel Trilling's liberalism to T.S. Eliot's conservatism; and although its presence in the media and on campuses was almost as thinly distributed as in society at large, it is still possible to speak of it as the cultural orthodoxy of the fifties and early sixties. As with its conceptual equivalent, modernization theory, in the disciplines of political science and economics, which charted the emergence of postcolonial societies, modernism in art and thought presupposed Western models (for all its attention to "primitive" art), optimistic expectations regarding experimentation and change, and high standards (with an appropriate perspectival relativism) in political and ethical judgments. These values—the sanctity of the individual, free inquiry and expression, social justice (variously defined), et cetera—were able to draw tacit assent from a wide spectrum of public opinion, even in the absence of theoretical clarity or a common program. Their esthetic equivalents—the organic unity of the work of art, personal vision, artistic freedom—gradually became the assumptions under which college courses in literature and other arts were taught, and by which even mass-circulation magazines portrayed the cultural work of the period.

Challenging this orthodoxy, a great wave of *antimodernism* broke in the late sixties and swept through the seventies. Much of its impetus came, of course, from antiestablishment sentiment generated by an unpopular war, but the mental changes at work in the new generation went well beyond both transient radicalism and temporary dropping out. Antimodernism expressed itself in the varied forms of primitivism and irrationalism flowering at the time, though these had long been present in modernism itself, an undercurrent that, like the return of the repressed, came to full consciousness only when its fearful contingencies were acted out, sometimes with appalling reductiveness and violence.[30] At the heart of these dark wisdoms was a change of mind or heart about the efficacy of modernization, material progress, and scientific advancement—in underdeveloped countries (as they were called at the time) and in developed ones as well—to satisfy the needs for personal intimacy, acceptance of deviance, and the like that became uppermost in importance. The parameters of progress, the authority of science, and leadership by all elites came under intellectual questioning and active challenge. The travails of the newly independent third-world nations were uniformly explained as consequences of an imperialism practiced under the name of Western enlightenment and universal values. "Power to the people" meant, in cultural terms that went beyond liberating parklands and resisting drug busts, an affirmation of folk cultures, peasant wisdom (sometimes linked to hallucinogenic drugs), and youthful innovations in style, morals, and occupation. Its most radical, indeed ingenious, move was to characterize even liberal tolerance, the hallmark of modern progressivism, as an instrument of oppression, as proclaimed by the disgruntled but still utopian Marxist Herbert Marcuse, who had never attracted so wide a political following as he did among the hippies.

Yet this, like other revolutions, ran through later, inevitably bathetic, phases. The embarrassing McGovern campaign, the winding down in Vietnam, and the failure or corruption of revolutions around the world took the afflatus out of antimodernism.[31] Marxist theoreticians continued to make a cottage industry out of revising predictions and courting alliances with marginal groups—in which they were abetted by basically apolitical intellectual adventurers such as the deconstructionists—but their influence was limited to college campuses, where they linger to this day. The empty space opened by apolitical apathy at the turn of the eighties was quickly filled by the greater energy of *postmodernism*. It converted political into cultural skepticism with a gusto and freedom of invention that made this sublimation seem a triumph rather than defeat.

Jeffrey Alexander describes the shift from politics to culture as the adoption of an alternative mythology: "If we consider postmodernism

as myth . . . we must deal with it as the successor ideology to radical
social theory, animated by the failure of reality to unfold in a manner
that was consistent with the expectations generated by that antimoder-
nization creed." Postmodernism's intellectual hallmarks—diminished expectations of reason in thought and practice, linguistic skepticism so
negative that it makes linguistic communication seem impossible, a lo-
calism that makes a mantra of "diversity," and other traits described by
one of its practitioners as "weak thought"—conspire to render all political aspirations merely provisional, like any other narrative. Alexander's
keen way of framing these familiar characterizations is to hint at the
tragicomedy implicit even in the densely textured prose of its master
thinkers. Postmodernism as myth finds fitting mottos in *Waiting for Godot*, the tragicomic artwork said to stand at its origin:

Estragon: I can't go on like this.

Vladimir: That's what you think.

. . .

Vladimir: Well? Shall we go?

Estragon: Yes, let's go.

They do not move.[32]

Selecting a motto for an entire cultural movement is, of course, a formula for distortion; the above pungently expresses the worldview of
postmodern art and thought but hardly accounts for their vigorous and
multitudinous forms of expression in the last decades of the century.
Postmodernism's hallmark irony pertains to none of its elements as viv-
idly as to the rise of the tendency itself: it appeared at a time of unprecedented prosperity, bountiful gains in public health and life expectancy,
and world political transformations that can be called without embarrassment the downfall of evil.[33] Another way of framing this paradox is
to ask, Why did the philosophy known as deconstruction, questioning
the possibility of adequate linguistic reference, appear precisely at the
onset of the communications revolution? What were the creators of literature, theater, and visual arts of the last decades of the century thinking when they provided an imagery of violent decay and a prevailing
sense of incoherence to a nation with rising median income, declining
poverty, waning racial inequality, growing educational quantity if not
quality, and other parameters of improving social welfare?[34]

A general answer to such questions would draw on considerable evidence from the history of the intelligentsia that a consistent portion of
this grouping is constitutionally disaffected and somewhat depressed by
social progress.[35] A more specific answer would turn on the observation
that the intelligentsia's counsels of despair appeared at the precise point

of a new class's emergence, a grouping delegated to work on public as well as private issues with tools more powerful than those the traditional intellectual would employ. Cultural and political despair at the state of the nation was a concomitant of the intelligentsia's awareness that it was, in its modernist and antimodernist forms, on the way out. Numerous reflections on this passage, with such titles as *Decline of the New* and *The Last Intellectuals* testify to this awareness. Its members have largely, in work practices and living habits, adapted themselves to the prevailing pragmatic ethos, though remaining inclined to morose delectation at continuing world woes.[36]

Although artists, critics, and other members of the intelligentsia made a handsome provision of cultural goods for the several social strata in the decades just past, the postmodern cornucopia of cultural fruits, with their emotional coolness and bitter aftertaste, could go only so far in stimulating the imagination of an increasingly self-confident and mainstream class. Although postmodernism performed an invaluable function for the New Class during this time, in validating its wide cultural curiosity and insouciant blending of varied experiences, their fortunes are not inevitably linked, and the temperamental differences between them are becoming increasingly marked. Although intellectuals both modern and postmodern are sunk in the mode of letting go—the title of the leftist art historian T.J. Clark's *Farewell to an Idea* is characteristic—the nation and its most energetic new class are moving on at a different tempo.[37]

Succeeding postmodernism's political and esthetic indulgence in the pleasures of melancholy, a new spirit has arisen in intellectual circles at home and abroad, substantial enough to constitute the trend that Alexander labels *neomodernism*. Now that capitalism, rechristened "the market," is the only economic game in the global village, not only financial but political and philosophical writers have been adopting thought modes that tend to validate its working principles. "Market realism" in economic theory, "public sphere" or "civil society" terminology in social thought, and "rational choice" models in political science indicate that modernism's liberal and individualist canons are being intensively renewed and refined.[38] Just as deconstruction and other postmodern philosophical currents issuing from France took measurable hold in Anglo-Saxon lands (less so in others), a later wave of French theoretical influence, whose common thread is an updating of the liberal tradition in politics and ethics, appears to be gaining a purchase.[39] And the turn in behavioral and psychological thinking toward a revival of neo-Darwinian genetic and physiology-based inquiry—though it runs counter to the liberal preference for nurture over nature in analysis and action—may well be related to the new realism of neomodernism.

There is, of course, no clean sweep in intellectual history. Remnants of the modern and the antimodern still show themselves amid the still resounding postmodern discourse, whereas neomodernist formulations are only beginning to crystallize as a coherent trend. The structure of cultural discourse, as we've observed, is derived from available logical oppositions such as these, and intellectuals' very existence draws life from the controversies they engender. But in an age of spreading acceptance of Western norms of democracy, human rights, and economic freedom as the only respectable ones—despite their difficulty in dealing with intractable poverty and mental darkness in Africa and Asia, and in the face of violent opposition by Moslem fundamentalists—it would be an overestimation of the authority of postmodernism to think that its burden of irony and nostalgia can long maintain credence.[40]

It is likely that the New Class, imbricated as it is with the business community and a force for rationalizing and maximizing the global marketplace, if it is not driving the turn toward neomodernist thinking, will be in ready sympathy with it. Nevertheless, the transition to a neomodernist orientation is sure to be accompanied by a persistence of postmodernist impulses and a lingering devotion to certain antimodernist sentiments, for example, distrust of industrialization and market forces as they affect the environment. Such messy affairs in the history of ideas may give trouble to intellectual historians, but this layered cultural discourse is likely to be readily assimilated by the New Class, whose mentality is itself fashioned in layers, showing commitments to classes above and below it and tastes for both the high and the low in the arts.

Another question that can receive no firm answer as yet concerns the consequences for the national welfare of the latest turns in the history of modernism and of the New Class's potential absorption in them. Since this class can only gain in prominence in the course of current economic trends—perhaps emerging to social dominance in the long run—its relations with other classes will require mutual adjustment, a portion of which will be acted out in the realm of culture. This emergent class is inherently malleable and educable, since its strength lies in its educational resources, and the latter, though primarily in technical and specialist spheres, spill over into cultural curiosity and participation. We may anticipate that its cultural openness will continue to encourage syntheses of popular and elite arts and adaptions of old forms to new needs and desires. But this is also a pragmatic and somewhat ruthless mentality, so that the nation can look forward to further disruptions in longstanding cultural practices, such as classical music genres and venues, which by current financial indications may eventually follow *Lieder* recitals into the dustbin of history. On the other hand (to stay within the range of this example), opera and dance will be encouraged to explore new compositional premises and performance modes, thus sustaining the experimental impulse of modernism and the inveterate human desire for novelty.

A more elusive, spiritual question remains to challenge the imagination: will the nation's fund of idealism, in political and social as well as cultural forms, be enlarged or diminished by the New Class's increasing prominence? We have been made aware of the low state of public confidence in almost all institutions and professions, and have also been apprised of twists and turns in this detachment, as national traumas have come and passed. Not as easily measurable is the influence the detached attitudes and shifting expressions of postmodern culture exert on the body politic, but it is surely present in some degree. The youthful vigor and self-confidence of the New Class may well bring about a break with the low estimations and expectations that postmodern culture has encouraged, though it may never recapture the idealism inspired by a Whitman or Lincoln, Roosevelt or King. In the following chapter, I scout the possibilities of cosmopolitanism as one such avenue of reinvigoration.

The mystification that both participants in and observers of the new grouping's culture must avoid is the bland supposition that it is a classless one. This class's rise to prominence in the social and economic sphere isn't calculated to lead to a relaxation of class antagonisms, as alarms raised about the increasing polarization of income groups already remind us. Nor is its cool cultural trolling likely to lead to stronger links to other classes and ethnicities. The restless shifts of art production and marketing, the ritualized celebration of rediscovered or freshly concocted ethnic works, the uncloseting of deviant taste and behavior at the margins of polite society and traditional culture—these are expressions not so much of democratic idealism as of an elite's fortification of itself with a set of recherché criteria for restricted entrance. Class positioning in this new culture is structured by the great divide between the arts establishment and a postmodern intelligentsia on the one hand, and the broad middle and lower classes on the other, with the New Class somewhat uncertainly finding its way to an identity between them. If the artistic and intellectual establishment is to effect a more democratic distrubution of cultural goods, it will have to do more than redistribute public and private moneys in a more equable ethnic and geographical coverage. It will be required to grasp and own up to the workings of class and even to speak its language.

NOTES

1. Good examples of each are, respectively, Gianni Vattimo, *The End of Modernity: Nihilism and Hermeneutics in Postmodern Culture*, trans. J.R. Snyder (Baltimore and London, 1988) and Ernest Gellner, *Reason and Culture: The Historic Role of Rationality and Rationalism* (Oxford and Cambridge, Mass., 1992).

2. This divided or dialectical relationship to tradition was set forth in a lecture

at Johns Hopkins University (Dec. 5, 1996) by a leading scholar of postmodern literature, Linda Hutcheon. She has no doubt developed it in print.

3. The broad subject of selfhood has been copiously set out in Charles Taylor, *Sources of the Self: The Making of the Modern Identity* (Cambridge, Mass., 1989).

4. Mark Crispin Miller, *Boxed In: The Culture of TV* (Evanston, Ill., 1988).

5. Rick Moody, "Surveyors of the Enlightenment" (review of Pynchon's *Mason & Dixon*), *Atlantic Monthly* (July 1997), p. 106.

6. Both the theorists and the practitioners of this kind of fiction have attained something like canonical status by the issuing of a Norton anthology: *Postmodern American Fiction*, eds. Paula Geyh, Fred G. Leebron, and Andrew Levy (New York and London, 1998).

7. David Brooks's *Bobos in Paradise: The New Upper Class and How They Got There* (New York, 2000) entertainingly describes these style preferences, which seem to constitute the bobo paradise itself.

8. Robert A.M. Stern, "The Postmodern Continuum," in W.J. Lillyman, M.F. Moriarty, and D.J. Neuman, eds., *Critical Architecture and Contemporary Culture* (New York and Oxford, 1994), p. 62.

9. The signature whiteness of Meier's buildings is incisively discussed—without, however, describing its classical allusions—in Barbara-Ann Campbell, *Paris: A Guide to Recent Architecture* (London, 1997), p. 198.

10. For later developments, see Diane Ghirardo, *Architecture after Modernism* (New York, 1996).

11. Irving Sandler, *Art of the Postmodern Era: From the Late 1960s to the Early 1990s* (New York, 1996).

12. A useful survey of this history is Peter Watson, *From Manet to Manhattan: The Rise of the Modern Art Market* (New York, 1992); the quotation that follows is from p. 419.

13. The million mark was passed in 1980, according to census figures cited in Diana Crane, *The Transformation of the Avant-Garde: The New York Art World, 1940–85* (Chicago and London, 1987), p. 4. By 1990 it had reached more than 1.6 million.

14. Quoted in Daniel Herwitz, *Making Theory/Constructing Art: On the Authority of the Avant-Garde* (Chicago and London, 1993), p. 232.

15. This was the judge's estimate in a case involving fair compensation for one of the estate's vultures: cited in Paul Alexander, *Death and Disaster: The Rise of the Warhol Empire and the Race for Andy's Millions* (New York, 1994), p. 244; the quotation that follows is from p. 243.

16. Tony Scherman, "Warhol: The Herald of Sampling," Arts and Leisure section, *New York Times* (Nov. 7, 1999), pp. 47, 49.

17. Louis Menand, "Finding It at the Movies" (review of Pauline Kael's *For Keeps*), *New York Review* (March 23, 1995), p. 17.

18. Abraham A. Moles, *Le kitsch: l'art du bonheur*, quoted in Matei Calinescu, *Faces of Modernity: Avant-Garde, Decadence, Kitsch* (Bloomington, Ind., and London, 1977), p. 258; the first emphasis is added. One merit of Moles's formulation is its recognition that kitsch operates not simply on mass society, as has been charged, but on meritocratic ones, where people are educationally disposed but not fully prepared to deal with cultural variety.

19. Camille Paglia, *Sexual Personae: Art and Decadence from Nefertiti to Emily*

Dickinson (New Haven and London, 1990); Wendy Steiner, *The Scandal of Pleasure: Art in an Age of Fundamentalism* (Chicago and London, 1995).

20. A caveat that applies here as elsewhere in these remarks: there are plenty of exceptions to these generalizations; only a masochist would relish the pleasure principle at work in the paintings of Anselm Kiefer or the installations of Joseph Beuys.

21. Pierre Bourdieu, *Distinction: A Social Critique of the Judgement of Taste*, trans. Richard Nice (Cambridge, Mass., 1984 [1979]), p. 360.

22. See, in addition to the series of neopragmatist works by Richard Rorty, Barbara Herrnstein Smith's *Belief and Resistance: Dynamics of Contemporary Intellectual Controversy* (Cambridge, Mass., 1997).

23. Works by Lasch mentioned here are better known than Eagleton's *Illusions of Postmodernism* (Oxford and Cambridge, Mass., 1996).

24. I use the term favored by an earlier generation of pragmatists, particularly as employed by Josiah Royce in *The Philosophy of Loyalty*. For a summary, see John Clendenning, *The Life and Thought of Josiah Royce* (Nashville and London, 1999 [1985]).

25. Wassily Kandinsky, *Über das Geistige in die Kunst*, in K.C. Lindsay and P. Vergo, eds. and trans., *Kandinsky: Complete Writings on Art* (London, 1982).

26. See, for example, Virginia Held, *Feminist Morality: Transforming Culture, Society, and Politics* (Chicago and London, 1993).

27. To the objection that irrationalism in art did not begin yesterday, one may argue that modern art, inspired by Freud, aimed at a systematic probing of the unconscious.

28. See Barbara Johnson, ed. *Freedom and Interpretation: The Oxford Amnesty Lectures 1992* (New York, 1993).

29. Jeffrey C. Alexander, *Fin de Siècle Social Theory: Relativism, Reduction, and the Problem of Reason* (London and New York, 1995); the quotation that follows is from p. 24.

30. Lionel Trilling's *Beyond Culture: Essays on Literature and Learning* (New York, 1965) was one of several texts to acknowledge these strains of modernism as chickens come home to roost.

31. Lingering sentiment for Castro's revolution, expressed in the campaign to end the United States embargo, is the last echo of these devotions.

32. Samuel Beckett, *Waiting for Godot: tragicomedy in 2 acts* (New York, 1954), p. 60.

33. A number of historical works dwelling on the notion that the United States is doomed to decline, if it hasn't already, appeared not only before but after the country's triumph in the cold war. For patterns of overexpansion and excessive military expenditure that testify to a coming decline, see Paul Kennedy, *The Rise and Fall of the Great Powers: Economic Change and Military Conflict from 1500 to 2000* (New York, 1987); for the view that it has already occurred, because of our foreign policy's preference for power over magnanimity, see Donald W. White, *The American Century: The Rise and Decline of the U.S. as a World Power* (New Haven and London, 1996).

34. For the statistics on these and other measures of progress, see Stephen Moore and Julian L. Simon, *It's Getting Better All the Time: 100 Greatest Trends of the Last 100 Years* (Washington, D.C., 2000). Measured by the data on crime,

divorce, and diverse educational outcomes, the national welfare doesn't, to be sure, look as good; these judgments are given a moralistic slant and political spin in such texts as William J. Bennett, *The Index of Leading Cultural Indicators: American Society at the End of the Twentieth Century* (New York and Colorado Springs, Colo., 1999 [1994]).

35. Beyond more general lambastings of intellectual habits of mind by Joseph Schumpeter, Edward Shils, et al., see Arthur Herman, *The Idea of Decline in Western History* (New York, 1997), for historical and recent examples of this syndrome.

36. For an up-to-date yet old-fashioned outpouring of intellectual *Weltschmerz*, apocalyptic and even survivalist, see Morris Berman, *The Twilight of American Culture* (New York and London, 2000).

37. T.J. Clark, *Farewell to an Idea, Episodes from a History of Modernism* (New Haven and London, 1999); the valedictory is not only to modernism but to its attendant ideas, expressed with a faint hope in the penultimate sentence that "the myth [of socialism] will survive its historic defeat."

38. See Alexander, p. 32 ff. for a summary of these scholarly schools.

39. For a sampling of these writings, see Mark Lilla, ed., *New French Thought: Political Philosophy* (Princeton, N.J., 1994).

40. Critical reestimates of what has come to be called "Eurocentrism" have served to blunt the force of the "postcolonial" radical attack on it: thus, expanding the sources of Western values beyond the Greeks, as in David Gress, *From Plato to NATO: The Idea of the West and Its Opponents* (New York, 1998), strengthens their foundations beyond narrow classicist supports; and Jared Diamond's biological-geographical explanation of the West's global dominance (*Guns, Germs, and Steel: The Fates of Human Societies* [New York and London, 1997]), designed to undercut racialist assumptions, only underscores the inevitability of its triumph, given its initial geographic and later technological advantages.

6

A Cosmopolitan Class?

Homer by divers reports may be ascribed to divers countries, and
indeed to the wise no country comes amiss.
—the sophist Calasiris

In my later teaching days, I would at times look up from my notes while
lecturing on modern literature and meet the attentive gaze of Jane Chen
or Tania Ng. During consultations they spoke without accent (one does
a Valley girl drawl to perfection) and were neatly groomed and unaf-
fectedly civil—well above the standard of Ms. Worthington and Ms.
Schapiro. They were touchingly interested in literature despite being, the
one pre-med, the other pre-engineering. It would repeatedly come to me
that they were accomplishing what I and others of my background were
up to in our time: without embarrassment or struggle, they were assim-
ilating beautifully. The one, daughter of a Chinese-American business-
man, the other, of a Vietnamese refugee, they were not merely entering
the professions but, by their mastery of computer technique, were destined for the New Class. Their far-flung origins and easy reorientation
toward a non-Western culture give their prospective entry into that
grouping a distinctive aspect: it has the makings of a cosmopolitan class.

From all appearances, these young people and others I've encountered
are not particularly eager to maintain a dual identity, though they are
as likely as not members of Asian-American or other ethnic student organizations, dutifully committed to honoring family rituals, and respon-

sive in providing items of Oriental lore to discussions of literature and life. By the same token, they seem unaware of their New Class destiny and use terms such as "middle class" and "mainstream" to describe their social aspirations. They wear their racial distinction as comfortably as their crisply ironed shorts and smartly arranged hairdos. The patterns of acculturation are proceeding here as neatly as the textbooks once prescribed, before a new historical ideology made the "melting pot" metaphor anathema.

Their assimilation is obviously eased by the attitudes of their contemporaries, the children of the "mainstream middle class" with whom they identify and who show no strain in adopting them as buddies. Just as important in creating this relaxed atmosphere as the liberal tolerance so strongly emphasized in schools and homes is the subtler but detectable taste for the exotic that colors this generation's social encounters. The Ms. Worthingtons and Ms. Schapiros don't attend group manifestations of what has been called, somewhat derisively, "symbolic ethnicity" out of mere dutifulness but with signs of relishing what's remote from their well-protected enclaves. The Far Eastern—and, it might be added, the Eastern European, Latin American and other—contingents on campus and in gathering places for highly educated young people are incubating a new wave of what only idealists have hitherto thought Americans capable: a world perspective. Although familiar aspects of the national culture have been subjected to the postmodern mix of irony and nostalgia, a more promising growth of *curiosity* about its unfamiliar components has also been in evidence. Cultural change is afoot at the level not merely of a style trend but of a collective mentality, and it behooves us to consider how New Class exposure to internationalism (in politics), globalism (in economics), exoticism (in taste), and other forms of worldliness may be advancing this potential transformation of America.

To assess the signs of this new mentality, a backward glance over earlier versions of a wider than national perspective is in order. After the great immigration waves of the late-ninteenth and early-twentieth centuries, the United States has been consistently celebrated—and self-celebrated ad nauseam—as a gathering of nations and a land of liberation. As most immigrants and immigration historians know, however, this ingathering of exiles was riven by conflict, not only between newcomers and earlier arrivals but within and between ethnic groups. The conditions that made previous historical instances of polyethnicity work fairly well—distinct groups' specialization in economic activity, whether as merchants, craftsmen, or laborers, and their recognized place in a hierarchical social space[1]—operated in American society only for an initiation period. The offspring of Irish navvies, Jewish seamstresses, and Scandinavian farmers became something other than traditional roles dictated. The co-presence of Irish and black navvies, Jewish and Italian seamstresses, and Scandinavian and German farmers produced mixed results in social harmony, but a growing restraint on overt prejudice and increased opportunities for occupational change made for a new kind of polyethnic society, the one we enjoy today for better or worse.[2]

Along with the rise of group self-consciousness, born of the anxieties of surviving in an alien medium and furthered by ethnic activists and institutions, there arose in the twentieth century's first decades an ideology of ethnic distinctiveness. This ideology, cultural pluralism, had from the outset divergent strains that have made the term "pluralism" a nest of contradictory implications. To this day, pluralism's offspring, multiculturalism, bears the marks of this twin heritage and cannot be discussed with full agreement on its principles. It is worthwhile to untangle both strains in these ideologies, for their logical incompatibility reveals the conflicting impulses that generate them.

The formal difference between the two pluralisms—which may be called, for short, Kallen pluralism and Bourne pluralism, after the authors of their founding statements—is readily summarized.[3] The one assumes that polyethnic societies survive as congeries of inveterately distinct entities; the other observes that social interaction, at least in the American context, is an inevitably and desirably synthetic process. On the one hand: because these ethnic groups are different from each other, they should be protected, by themselves and others, in order to remain so. On the other: because these ethnic groups are different from each other, they tend both to repel others and to attract curiosity, even desire, so that in interpersonal relations they produce not only mixed offspring but cultural creations that could not have been dreamed of by each of them alone.

Horace M. Kallen's statement of the first option, *Culture and Democracy in the United States* (1924) received a number of modifications over the years, so that comparisons between earlier and later versions of his thesis have become fertile territory for students of the developing concept. Recent commentary has focused on an uncomfortable strain in Kallen's thought, the racialism implicit in his notion of essential differences between races, nationalities, and other putative entities. These categories and the very notion of fixed differences are historical and ideological constructs, as the New Historicism maintains. Moreover, the idea that the ethnics are "unmeltable" and not only cannot but should not lose their identity has become a useful banner for ethnic claims to political influence.[4] Yet the most serious shortcoming of Kallen pluralism may be neither its essentialist premises nor its easy reduction into a rationale for interest group politics but its provincialism—the latter-day version of an earlier American provinciality that is today looked back on as a mere growth stage.

Kallen's later effort in the *Cultural Pluralism and the American Idea*[5] to meld ethnic diversity with cosmopolitan ideals is touching but pointless, given his premises—the natural "organic whole" of local groups and the social utility of maintaining boundaries between them. His faith that increased education will lead group members to become "no stranger in any different country and culture" comes a bit late in the day, after a lifetime's encouragement of individuals to cherish and preserve their cultural birthrights. The mantra of diversity—in Kallen's rhetoric it attains the drumbeat of "diverse utterances of diversities"—promises only an agglutination of distinct entities, suggested even in his formula of a "concrete intercultural total which is the culture of America." Unlike the ethnic groups, which are by nature organically unified, the national culture can aspire only to be the material sum of their spiritually endowed artifacts.[6]

Kallen was more enthusiastic when describing American culture not as a mere sum total but as an abundant and nurturant reservoir (his equivalent of the prevalent metaphors of soup, salad bowl, et cetera). Yet his belated effort to acknowledge the vitality of synthetic as well as constituent cultures shows little awarenes of the processes of cultural interaction and cosmopolitan transcendence. In contrast, Randolph Bourne's 1916 essay, "Trans-National America,"[7] is now highly regarded, but approbation of its multicultural stance has blunted its potential to correct today's version. Bourne, like recent multiculturalists, was in no doubt that Americanization offered "a higher ideal than the 'melting-pot' " (p. 179), but unlike theirs, his was "a new cosmopolitan ideal" (p. 180). He saw America as standing in need of a better culture than its persistently provincial one. The "ruling class" (p. 180), largely Anglo-Saxon, had by its cultural narrowness failed in one of its national aspirations: the founders and their successors never "succeeded in transforming the colony into a real nation, with a tenacious, richly woven fabric of native culture" (p. 181). This paean to diversity makes not mere inclusiveness but synthetic transformation of local cultures the basis for a national culture—one well on the way toward international consciousness. Cosmopolitanism in this light is no mere gilding on either ethnic or national culture but a necessary aspiration of the latter.

So edifying an ideal, operating in the face of a cultural scene that Bourne regarded within some disdain, is to be pursued by raising the quality of cultural products and practices. In contrast to current pop intellectuals, Bourne was no friend of "the American culture of the cheap newspaper, the 'movies,' the popular song, the ubiquitous automobile" (p. 182). In an age of strident patriotism, he judged that "America has as yet no impelling integrating force" (p. 183), for this would have to be a cultural rather than a political ideal. It was to be achieved in the arts, given the evidence that in some at least of "the finer forms—music, verse, the essay, philosophy—the American genius puts forth work equal to any of its contemporaries" (p. 184). But Bourne's estimate of American drama and fiction was a low one and, given the limited evidence of high achievement in other arts (in reaction to which Pound and Eliot were at that time in the process of emigrating), whence came Bourne's confidence that his paradoxical prophecy—"our American cultural tradition lies in the future" (p. 184)—would come to fulfillment?

Bourne's prediction was predicated on overcoming American provincialism through a stronger sense of the larger world. What was needed was not simply "a cosmopolitan federation of national colonies, of foreign cultures," but "a new orientation of the American mind in the world" (p. 185). He was attentive to signs that our colleges and universities were promoting an international mentality through the teaching of the humanities, and in this he anticipated the formative influence on the educated classes of systematic curricula, like the Columbia and Chicago great books courses.[8] Bourne was perhaps at his most inspired in prophesying, if not precisely the New Class, the rise of an international mentality akin to that class's.

Although he employs the metaphors of integration that have become familiar in multiculturalism—the interweaving of "many threads of all sizes and colors" (p. 187), though not the rainbow, the salad bowl, and the mongrelism—Bourne's more strenuous drive is toward forming a new kind of dual consciousness. It is not that of the immigrant (or, in W.E. Du Bois's version, of the African-American) but that of the citizen of both America and the world: "Dual [ethnic/national] citizenship we may have to recognize as the rudimentary form of that international citizenship to which, if our words mean anything, we aspire" (p. 186). Although it does not specify the reeducation of the intelligentsia as a requirement for this transformation, the essay ends with an appeal to the rising generation: "To make real this striving amid dangers and apathies is work for a younger *intelligentsia* of America" (p. 188). In a confusion for which both major and minor prophets may be forgiven, it is not clear from Bourne's vision whether we have yet to achieve this "Beloved Community" or are already there, if only we knew it: "Already we are living this cosmopolitan America. What we need is everywhere a vivid consciousness of the new ideal" (p. 188).

* * *

Are we? Do we? If Kallen pluralism and Bourne pluralism represent polar types, toward which of these poles has turn-of-the-millennium America been moving? Little enthusiasm is shown of late for any collective ideal that entails American leadership in a federation among the nations. The international involvements of recent decades have usually been supported or not supported by populace and parties as they've been urged by relevant ethnic groups along entirely predictable lines: African-Americans enthusiastic for the South African boycott; Jewish community groups vying for diplomatic influence on Israel/Palestine issues; Serbian-Americans outraged by NATO bombing in the Kosovo conflict—the latter a rare instance of deviation between general and specific publics. Bourne pluralism's challenge—that to have a mature national consciousness we must develop not only a polyethnic but also an international consciousness—has been superseded by a worthy but more limited goal, apportioning recognition and rewards to racial and ethnic claimants.

Yet the crystallization of a global economy has inevitably fostered awareness of the larger world, since a global perspective shared by the adepts of international communications and enterprise cannot be restricted to market watching and exchange-rate arbitrage alone. One of the questions suggested by Bourne's challenge to the "intelligentsia" is how the latest entrants to that grouping from the New Class will respond to it, if at all. Another, narrower question involves the leading lights of the intelligentsia: how far and in what ways will American intellectuals perform a leadership role in developing a cosmopolitan consciousness?[9]

In common with American society at large, the New Class is responsive to the narratives and claims of the multicultural campaigners, and institutions staffed by the intelligentsia (higher education, the arts establishment, the media) are among the most vigorous exponents of ethnic "diversity." Yet there are signs that stalwarts of postmodern thinking are coming to acknowledge the desirability of a broader international perspective: "cosmopolitanism" has become a much heard term in political, literary, and philosophical discourse. It would be worthwhile to assess the varieties of this usage, since they not only map an intellectual trend but allow the New Class's place in it to stand out more clearly. In a summary view, the positions in this field may be categorized as anthropological, philosophical, and political.

The *anthropological* variant, that which most clearly emerges from postmodernist thinking, is perhaps best recognized by its key term, "hybridity." Though presented, in the prose of such theoreticians as Homi K. Bhabha and Gayatri C. Spivak, with a rhetoric that suggests deliberate mystification, the burden of this approach is clear enough.[10] It goes beyond the ritualized celebration of differences to test and ultimately to undermine the notion of difference itself. Rather than focusing on the usual oppositions between first- and third-world nations, colonialists and the colonized, whites and people of color, this inquiry searches out liminal situations, "sites" where new identities in both camps are shaped by interaction. With an insight into the mutual influences and consequent changes affecting all participants in colonial and postcolonial encounters, this perspective offers valuable encouragement to think of ourselves, on both sides of color lines and cultural divides, as hybrid and complex, and by that token as potential members of a world community.

No one will gainsay the virtues of this position, tending as it does to undermine the self-satisfied sense of difference that marks oppressors and oppressed on both the national and international scenes. Yet recognizing the multiple strains in any identity should be accompanied by a realistic awareness of the difficulties and dangers inherent in all such liminal positions. Anthropological cosmpolitanism makes an implicit claim that the transcendent synthesis of Bourne pluralism is readily available since we are all already hybrid. Although the patterns of ethnic intermarriage and cultural interaction among European-origin groups and between them and Asian-origin groups are working to move the New Class and others in this direction, these trends are not uniformly strong for all minorities. Given the apparently intractable resistances to full black and Native American amalgamation, the achievement of a national and international perspective is not significantly furthered by the observation that ethnicities and individuals are not much different since all are compound.

Bhabha's native India, with its rigid internal divisions yet enduring vitality, illustrates on a national scale the double-entry bookkeeping required in assessing polyethnic or multinational hybridity. On a personal scale, the gains and losses likely to be incurred by hybrid individuals are dramatically illustrated by the career of novelist Salman Rushdie. Indian, Pakistani, and English by turns (and currently an American resident), inspired in art and life by cultural lore and lifestyles drawn from multiple sources, Rushdie also fulfills the image of cosmopolitan man in his extreme enactment of the fate of the deracinated *Luftmensch*. Now returned to almost normal status, after years spent in isolation and embittered self-examination, he remains the postmodern, postcolonial intellectual par excellence, enjoying the rewards of superb and influential esthetic achievements and suffering the misery of latent worldwide anathematization in Islam.[11] One can only conclude that hybridity doesn't make a cosmopolitan stance any easier.

Another basis that has recently been invoked for cosmopolitanism is the *philosophical*. This discourse goes back to the ancient Sophists and Stoics (as the epigraph to this chapter recalls) and received its modern form in the Enlightenment, particularly in the formulations of Immanuel Kant. In response to the depravities being committed under the name of nationalism, which are sometimes justified by invoking the norms of local cultures and their distinct value systems, a number of recent philosophers have revived Enlightenment ideas of a universal human nature and the ethical absolutes that flow from it. These philosophical proponents of universal human rights and norms have been charged with elitism, for their cosmopolitanism seems based on a standard of rationality that ignores the culturally inflected reasonings of local groups. Indeed, the latest version of cultural relativism, postmodernist antifoundationalism, makes it impossible for many current intellectuals to accept the abstract principles involved in this line of thought, even when they are inclined to make the ethical and political judgments it entails. Thus universalistic thinking has been reduced by its opponents to merely another Eurocentric and ideologically tainted imposition on the minds and acts of others around the globe.

Efforts to reconcile the universal and the local—to rescue nationalism, sacrosanct during the decolonization period, from the stains it has recently acquired—have also proceeded apace. Postmodern intellectuals such as Julia Kristeva have—as her title *Nations Without Nationalism* suggests—urged us to dissociate its wholesome (self-expressive and thus universal) and unwholesome (atavistic, inward-looking) impulses.[12] Other philosophers such as Martha C. Nussbaum have been stalwart in upholding the universal human rights of, for example, third-world women as superseding those of regional cultures.[13] In place of the anthropological view that sees racial and ethnic fusions moving toward widespread likeness, the philosophical position assumes an initial and indelible human nature. It speaks, on the basis of factors that all humans share, of principles by which all should act and judge. Although agreement about, for example, United Nations accords on universal human rights and international conventions on war crimes may command general, though at times grudging, acceptance, it is difficult at this stage of intellectual history to expect broad agreement on a human norm as the basis of humane values. Too many members of the intelligentsia in both first- and third-world lands have too many reservations about abstract ideas of human nature to allow them standing as political and ethical norms.

A useful step toward making cosmopolitanism a practical rather than abstract philosophical position would be a recognition that, as an ethical stance involving worldwide attentiveness and obligation, it makes large, perhaps excessive demands on would-be cosmopolitans. Like the Judeo-Christian imperative to transcend self-love and Buddhist respect for the sanctity of all living things, the cosmopolitan ideal may be too exalted for everyday compliance. Just as the liberal imagination stems from impulses of benignity and enlightenment unimpeachable in themselves but fraught with temptations to sentimentality and self-satisfaction, a cosmopolitan perspective is vulnerable to bland philanthropy and permissive relaxation of standards for specially favored cases. A stern assessment of its rigors was made in the aftermath of its degradation by the mass criminality of World War II:

The appeal of tribal isolation and master race ambitions was partly due to an instinctive feeling that mankind, whether a religious or humanistic ideal, implies a common sharing of responsibility.... [T]he idea of humanity, purged of all sentimentality, has the very serious consequence that in one form or another men must assume responsibility for all crimes committed by men, and that eventually all nations will be forced to answer for the evil committed by all others. Tribalism and racism are very realistic, if very destructive, ways of escaping this predicament of common responsibility.[14]

Whatever the accuracy of Hannah Arendt's explanation of the psychological roots of imperialism and fascism, her positive imperatives carry a Dostoyevskian ring that challenges contemporary accommodations. Whether derived from religious or secular humanist sources, an ethical stance that carries the world on its shoulders runs against the current of postmodernist thinking.

A third form of recent intellectual cosmopolitanism is the *political*. Since cosmopolitanism in itself has come to seem no hindrance to a variety of political ambitions, the wind has gone out of charges that it is inherently apolitical or even reactionary. Erstwhile Marxist thinkers such as Étienne Balibar have proposed that adopting a non-Marxist internationalism might substitute for world revolution as a liberatory ideal.[15] A number of radical intellectuals disappointed with political action on a national scale have turned to the broader though vaguer prospects of international action, labeling as empire the latest version of an old bête noire, "empire."[16]

Yet nothing comes without struggle on the left. Suspicion regarding cosmopolitans has a perdurable life not only on the right, given their implicit estrangement from religious assumptions and community obligations, but also on the left, given their propensity toward disengagement from partisan politics. The appearance of anticosmopolitanism in such works as Timothy Brennan's *At Home in the World: Cosmopolitanism Now*[17] suggests that the "politically correct" coalition of left-leaning tendencies, largely confined to the academy, is losing cohesion even there. As one critic observes, "What we now see, it seems, is a backlash against cosmopolitanism within the very subculture [of academic intellectuals] that has traditionally had most to gain from delocalization."[18]

The cosmopolitan trend remains an appealing option for many in the intelligentsia disabused of national and international ideologies yet unwilling to surrender a sense of political obligation. This degree of commitment shows itself in recent street protests against multinational institutions and corporations, some vulnerable to charges of labor abuse and environmental degradation. Yet the extreme selectivity of these denunciations—third-world standards of child labor and environmental practice being attacked only when a well-known brand name can be attached to them—has hardly contributed to the probity of this mini-movement. Nor have intellectuals been deeply engaged in it, whether by scholarly or organizational work with political impact.[19] It is difficult to recall a period when the normally *engagé* have been so silent: a series of foreign wars were fought by U.S. troops, using highly destructive technologies, in third-world and formerly second-world lands in the 1990s, with no more than a mild stir of complaint by antiwar groups and other descendants of the Vietnam protest era. Even the left-leaning intellectual response to the antiterrorism war is, beyond a spate of campus teach-ins, notable for its lack of contact with already constituted dissenting forces such as religious pacifists and civil-liberties groups. It is a strange cosmopolitanism, indeed, that flaunts its kinship with all races and its imaginative sympathy with all cultures, yet exhibits a perhaps well-founded despair of changing anything by political action or even rhetoric.

Leadership roles in a highly skeptical age are, of course, difficult for intellectuals, as well as politicians, to maintain. The charge of elitism is, perhaps, the one that most rankles much-abused postmodern intellectuals such as Gayatri Spivak and Edward W. Said, disturbing their high standing in postcolonial circles. Ad hominem thrusts—in these cases, of the expatriates' excessive distance from Indian women's lives and from Palestinian exigencies on the ground—are a staple of this criticism. The charge goes beyond questioning whether these cosmopolitans' successful participation in Western discourses can produce anything but reinforcement of Western values and unwitting support for Western dominance. It invokes their successful personal careers—and their allegorizing of those careers as emblematic of third-world progress—as testimony that individualistic drives remain urgent in maintaining a cosmopolitan perspective. The stick used to beat rootless cosmopolitans was for long their isolation and vulnerability; it has now been exchanged for one labeled "careerism" and "celebrity." The position of a leading recent exponent of cosmopolitanism, Bruce Robbins, is undoubtedly the most honest as well as the most limited: to intellectuals, he recommends "planetary expansiveness of subject-matter, on the one hand, and . . . unembarrassed acceptance of professional self-interest, on the other."[20]

* * *

Although they omit the traditional shibboleths of the brotherhood of man, these cosmopolitan trends cannot refrain from a normative and sometimes hortatory rhetoric. Both the anthropological and philosophical approaches purport to base themselves on the observed realities of hybridity and interconnection, yet cannot refrain from recommending what ought to be rather than what is. In our relativistic age, there is little chance that ethical absolutes can ground a cosmopolitan vision. In the absence of a widely agreed-upon basis for high ideals or political aspirations, the current approaches must content themselves with gingerly formulations and rather timid hopes. Schiller's "Ode to Joy" as sung in Beethoven's Ninth Symphony may be raised as an anthem in gatherings of the European Union, which is making some headway toward transnational unity, but is unlikely to stir Americans with other than esthetic inspiration.

There is, to be sure, some basis for a realistic cosmopolitanism to be found in recent evolutionary and genetic science, which has strongly supported a shift from divisive racial categorizing to affirming the oneness of human populations. The "out of Africa" thesis that traces the entire species back to an "African Eve" has fostered a literal sense of human brotherhood, although its interpretation of the evidence contained in the worldwide distribution of mitochondrial DNA is still disputed in specialist circles. This view has, moreover, been strengthed by the near-conquest of the human genomic code, bolstering the idea (long maintained by anthropologists on weaker evidence) that all people share a preponderance of the features that mark our species.

The actual data are more complex: according to a *New York Times* summary (Aug. 22, 2000), worldwide studies of neutral genetic markers—so-called "junk DNA"—show that 88 to 90 percent of differences between individuals occur within local populations, whereas 10 to 12 percent fall outside and may hold distinctions between races. As for the more significant genes encoding proteins that control bodily functions, some show no variability, some are varied but not correlated with race, and some—including those involving pigmentation, susceptibility to certain illnesses and, to some degree, performance on intelligence tests—are racially variable. Another summary puts the matter thus: biologists distinguish subspecies as geographic populations having +30 percent genetic difference, but traditional "races" have roughly 15 percent genetic difference and so are not subspecies. Yet physical expressions of these differences are sufficient to permit taxonomic determinations relevant in forensic identification and in anthropological studies of prehistoric migrations.[21] The science runs parallel with a rise in neo-Darwinian and other nature-over-nurture psychological theories that emphasize the functionalism and consequent universality of certain behavior patterns and values in the erotic and other interpersonal spheres. By a curious unexpected outcome, the feminist research purporting to document and explain—and thereby validate—differences between the sexes in performance and priorities also falls in with an enhanced awareness of universal behavior patterns. But this growing body of evidence has yet to be cautiously marshaled by the latest advocates of cosmopolitanism and it remains undeveloped in its cultural implications.

* * *

If anthropological cosmopolitanism's proposal of a hybrid status for much of humanity proves too weak a staff to sustain many a hybrid but alienated individual; if philosophical cosmopolitanism, for all its rational and noble claims for universal moral obligation, is unlikely to engage many in the relativistic postmodern intelligentsia; if political cosmopolitanism, trailing clouds of *bien-pensant* radicalism, can only weakly attract the disappointed survivors of that tradition, what source of feeling or belief could motivate a cosmopolitan renewal on the current cultural scene?

Operating conceptually among the discourses that alternately play down and play up racial, sexual, and other differences, the American intelligentsia has tried to maintain its responsiveness to issues broader than the local, untrammeled by the no longer compelling rhetoric of human brotherhood. Its New Class members are also eager to ward off accusations of mere dilettantism for the wide span of their cultural curiosity, without commiting themselves to a political concern for the people of those cultures—one that seems outmoded and encumbered by humanitarian sentimentality. Can they, can we, do better than formulating bumper-sticker slogans of the "think globally/act locally" variety? Can a realistic hope for cosmopolitanism be based on demonstrable behaviors and attitudes that emerge almost inevitably from new developments in the economic and technological spheres?

What form of cosmopolitanism would, for example, accord with the rising tide of individualism occurring in the first and even second of the global "worlds"? Even to put the issue in this way runs against the grain of recent thinking that notes this tide with alarm, condemning the self-indulgence and lack of concern for the community that it often entails. Communitarians of various stripes have been reminding us of the primacy of social obligations, and spokesmen for the ethnicities have strongly asserted the inescapability and self-enriching power of group identity. From a communitarian standpoint, individuals asserting universal rights—for example, of women from the third world who continue to be constrained in first-world countries to which their families migrate—embarrassingly complicate the problem. Yet there is reason to think that cosmopolitan perspectives stand a better chance of being nurtured by the spread of personal freedom than by the collective interests of groups and nations.

The chances for isolated individuals to foster in others a supple and inclusive worldview may seem limited, given the well-known vulnerability of loners within the ethnic and national systems that have long prevailed. If any thoughts of entirely transcending the narrow claims of national or group affiliation should tempt the would-be cosmopolitan, Hannah Arendt reminds us of the fate of stateless people (like herself, for a time during the war) when deprived of national identity and state support: "If a human being loses his political status, he should according to the implications of the inborn and inalienable rights of man, come under exactly the situation for which the declarations of such general rights provided. Actually the opposite is the case. It seems that a man who is nothing but a man has lost the very qualities which make it possible for other people to treat him as a fellow-man."[22] The fate of the Rushdies in recent persecutions brings these dire consequences up to date in the postcolonial, postmodern world. It is not the mass victims of holocausts but isolated individuals with excommunicating adversaries who today stand as exemplars of cosmopolitan vulnerability. But the worldwide response to Rushdie's victimization—even in Moslem lands where divergent interpretations of the Koranic tradition are tolerated— has been a testament to heightened concern for personal rights. Not only did Britain and other countries place an individual's protection ahead of nation-to-nation threats and potential advantages, and not only did publishers acting singly and in concert (and under dire threats in several cases fulfilled) promulgate the disapproved text, but many around the world perceived a religious and national community's trampling on personal expression as an anachronistic outrage. With fundamentalism of this breed active, all were alerted to the mentality, if not the scale, of the massive attacks on Western freedom that followed.

The affirmation of personal freedom was, no doubt, strongest in advanced industrial nations where human development measures such as longevity and literacy rank highest and where, by these criteria, it is possible to speak meaningfully of respect for the individual. Even in these regions, a cosmopolitan perspective is a luxury that even the best endowed, culturally and financially, sometimes find difficult to afford. Yet affluence affects perspectives not only in economic and political but in cultural and ethical matters. The reinvigoration of ethnicity in the second half of the twentieth century has been linked not to the earlier collective defensiveness or later political assertiveness of marginal groups but to the rising fortunes of many erstwhile immigrants. As John Higham puts it, "cultural pluralism would appeal to people who were already strongly enough positioned to imagine that permanent minority status might be advantageous. . . . Accordingly, cultural pluralism proved most attractive to people who were already largely assimilated. It was itself one of the products of the American melting pot."[23] The next step for their descendants, especially when ethnic roots are mixed, is to favor neither one or another group but ethnic culture itself: to celebrate the colorful and distinctive wherever one finds it. Receptivity to the artistic values of local cultures, whether of nearby neighborhoods or from around the globe, is already a step toward a cosmopolitan attitude to their deeper values.

The New Class would seem well positioned to advance in this direction. Stemming from diverse ethnic and class origins, its members have achieved the kind of financial and social solidity that enables open-minded encounters and often intimate linkages among people of diverse backgrounds. Their normal international communications, whether by travel or via the Internet, continually reinforce this receptivity. They are programmed by their work environments to favor the economic version of internationalism, placing the principle and opportunities of free trade somewhat ahead of labor-movement and environmentalist concerns. Yet they are far better informed about cultural patterns abroad than were previous generations of overseas entrepreneurs, and more fully aware of the global consequences of economic development in other than economic spheres.

This latest version of an educated class mentality represents the strongest force for cosmopolitanism in our time. With the widespread loss of confidence in the United Nations as a unifying institution and the withering of socialist internationalism, the forms of cosmopolitanism that long animated the Western intelligentsia have all but vanished. As segments of the labor movement, antidevelopment environmentalists, and latter-day young radicals reveal their Luddite limitations by opposing expanded international trade with the bugaboo of "globalization," the New Class replaces them as the best currently available hope for an active cosmopolitan stance toward an integrating world. The open question remains whether its members' economics-based perspective will be sufficiently attentive to worldwide social, human-rights, and environmental issues to fulfill the high responsibility laid down by our ethical prophets.

If any class or other grouping were called on to meet such challenges by its own devices alone, it might reasonably object to so exceptional a status. Fortunately, a number of global trends not only in trade and communications but in politics and law are working to support the New Class's inclinations in this direction. Not only the international scale of Internet communication but the emergence of English as a lingua franca furthers the American branch of this class in establishing links to its opposite numbers in developed and developing nations. The normalization of foreign travel not only in tourism but on regular business, as well as the increased frequency of long-term overseas assignments within corporate, governmental, and humanitarian organizations, makes for a culturally sophisticated leadership group like none in previous American history. The increased acceptance in law and public opinion of continued ties between Americans and their families' lands of origin moves in the same direction: not only are federal regulations more tolerant of claims for dual nationality but it became possible in the last decade for naturalized American citizens to serve as foreign minister of Bosnia and army commander in Lithuania. (We hear much of multinational corporations, but it becomes increasingly necessary to take account of multinational individuals.) Rather more than the dual consciousness advocated by traditional ethnic pluralists, new forms of dual identification emerging from international economic and political activities strengthen the basis for cosmopolitan perspectives.

These opportunities for self-definition hold an obvious attraction for members of the New Class, marked as it is by the individualistic urges regularly decried by community spokesmen and communitarian thinkers. The postmodern style of designing one's identity from a grab bag of personal preferences, ethnic, religious, even national, is nowhere more in evidence than in this grouping. It seizes on the freedom to move beyond one's group-assigned identity increasingly underwritten not only in public acceptance but in international law and practice. In a legal study titled *The Empowered Self*, free of the New Age claptrap usually associated with such phrases, Thomas M. Franck has collected the evidence that "the previously ineluctable hold on us of the old deterministic, communally imposed identitites—territorial, tribal, ethnic, racial, religious and linguistic—has begun to loosen."[24] Although Franck's speculative "new stage of human evolution in which loyalty to the state is transformed into a higher loyalty to humanity, symbolized by global (or regional) institutions of government, commerce, education, and communications," may be too much for even a cosmopolitan to hope, "the dawning of a notion that identity, whatever its manifestation, is a *personal* attribute" accords well with the inclinations and behavior of New Class people around the world. His evidence confirms the successful spread of "a series of more specific claims: to choose one's own nationality or nationalities, as well as trans-nation affinities, to select one's preferred name and that of one's children, to follow, or not follow, any religion as a matter of personal conscience, to pursue a chosen occupation, and even to select one's sex or gender." The wider public and legal acceptance of transsexuals and of unorthodox personal names does not mean that greater freedom necessarily constitutes a boon for cosmopolitanism, but awareness and tolerance of willed difference and principled commitment to individual rights are essential elements of that mentality.

* * *

A cosmopolitanism based on the relatively few multinational individuals among us might be long in coming; closer at hand may be a cosmopolitanism derived from the renewed polyethnic vitality around us. With the latest migrations from the Orient, Eastern Europe, and Latin America, the American melting pot continues to function and, with all its lapses from purity, should remain a standard for the world. The theoretical possibilities of this latest wave's movement beyond ethnicity toward a wider perspective have been sketched by David A. Hollinger in his *Postethnic America*.[25] Taking up the twin strands of pluralism associated with the names Kallen and Bourne, he urges that the latter provides a template for transcending the "pluralist-cosmopolitan tension found in multiculturalism," since Bourne's is "an alliance of pluralism and cosmopolitanism" (p. 11). While focusing on these intellectual implications, Hollinger pays less heed to the potentiality of recent immigrant waves to embody this new form of double consciousness in their own experience. As the new immigrants take up positions in a society already constituted as a stable ethnic mixture, they are less likely to reproduce previous patterns of defensive enclosure, and may well become exemplary in combining a sense of their local positioning with a measure of the worldliness they bring from differing points of origin.

This supple mind-set is not, of course, inevitable or easily come by. As Hollinger says, "cosmopolitanism is willing to put the future of every culture at risk through the sympathetic but critical scrutiny of other cultures, [while] pluralism is more concerned to protect and perpetuate particular, existing cultures" (p. 85). Given the stresses facing all immigrants, some avoidance of risk by protecting the traditional is to be anticipated. But pluralism's inward-looking impulse may no longer be as necessary for "postethnic" America as it was in the heyday of immigration and the nativism that resisted it. Despite recent ethnic and racial flare-ups in New York, Los Angeles, and other cities, the massive presence of cultural variety calls up attentiveness to other groups, mutual comparison and criticism (including self-criticism), and opportunities for relaxed mingling. What is true for the evolution of groups also holds for the development of individuals, Hollinger notes: "A truly postethnic America would be one in which the ethno-racial component in identity would loom less large than it now does in politics as well as culture, and in which affiliation by shared descent would be more voluntary than prescribed in every context" (p. 129). How far this process of self-definition will spread beyond the New Class, which is already so inclined, is one of the open but hopeful questions for America's future.

The impediments to such a risky and open-ended process are both universally human and specifically historical: culture is bound to be conservative, with tradition its very substance, and individuals hold fast to it as a source of stability, backed by their ancestors and self-confident in passing on their heritage. The late-twentieth-century cultural invigoration of various ethnicities was, moreover, strengthened by their palpable political and economic advances, and cynics will charge that the latter interests were what motivated the cultural campaigns. The conservative tendencies in social psychology and the motivating factors in recent history may not, however, be the only forces shaping a new sense of ethnicity. Postmodernist theory, insofar as it is a latter-day version of a long tradition of historicist thinking, has reminded us that not only nations but races and ethnicities are not naturally fixed but historically evolving—"socially constructed," in the current jargon. Just as groups abroad differ in their rates of change, as the variety of behavior patterns in the former Yugoslavia have demonstrated, so do American ethnicities show varied forms of evolution. American Jews, for example, have been accused of losing their identity and thus accomplishing the dissolution of Jewry that the Holocaust failed to achieve, but another view of their development might put their relaxed assimilation more positively and certainly less crudely. Other ethnicities have shown greater transformation and intergroup affinity than ethnic theorists have credited them with, so that the assimilation process—the formation, for example, of the grand "European-American" mixture that Richard Alba has studied—continues its daily work without paying lip service to the "melting pot." Although collective ideology, rhetoric, and interests continue to dominate the discourse, people's behavior belies history and theory with sudden, if inconsistent, gestures of cooperation, attraction, and empathy.

This may be because individuals in the late modern or postmodern world are not constituted quite as ethnic theory would have them. The legal theorist Jeremy Waldron has convincingly argued that the cosmopolitan version of the self—he uses Rushdie's terms for his own experience, "hybrid," "mongrel," even "bastard"—is the way in which identities are now characteristically formed and not, as posited by a series of communitarian theorists he discusses, as a creation of the community in which they are raised.[26] If the continued strength of genetic or early domestic influences be asserted, Waldron affirms that "the hybrid lifestyle of the true cosmopolitan is in fact the only appropriate response to the modern world in which we live" (p. 763)—that is, that even granted the strength of communal conditioning, a cosmopolitan flexibility in shaping oneself in response to others is necessary today. To the evident objection that such fluidity carries the dangers of psychic deracination and political vulnerability, Waldron suggests that these are problems that call for thoughtful skills: "Such integrity as the cosmopolitan individual has therefore requires *management*. Cultural structures cannot provide that management for [him or] her because too many of them are implicated in [his or] her identity, and they are too differently shaped" (p. 789). In a world of multiple influences, only a democratic rather than a hierarchical model of the self is adequate to the changefulness and complexity of life: "suppose we think about personal identity, not in terms of hierarchical management, but in terms of the democratic self-government of a pluralistic population" (p. 791).

It would be footless to suggest that members of the New Class are the only postmoderns capable of managing a synthetic identity. Management of the self has been going on for a long time, as Ian Hunter's work has demonstrated, and is an active though extraordinarily difficult process in communal societies faced by modernization, as the novels of Chinua Achebe and the plays of Wole Soyinka bear out. But this class may sport certain advantages in pursuit of controlled personal flexibility: its members are not only drawn from diverse backgrounds but are, many of them, diverse in background. It is synthetic and unfolding both on the individual and the collective scale. Nor should a number of its members' training in management, recruitment, and related personnel skills be lightly regarded as potential assets in defining a cultural identity. The practices of risk evaluation, of mutually beneficial negotiation, and of applying information to even the most qualitative of problems have a bearing on informal as well as business life. Above all, the New Class's self-confidence, together with the financial security to sustain it, may be relied on to help resist the imperatives of group identity, for such people have the will and means to choose in every other aspect of life and are unlikely to submit easily to any collective will, especially as the latter is interpreted by other individuals.

Perhaps a personal anecdote will not come amiss in describing New Class self-determination (although my demographics don't place me squarely in that rubric). On a recent visit to Israel, as I approached the Wailing Wall, a man of my generation of whom I asked directions asked in his turn, "Are you Jewish?" When I replied, "Formerly," he asked, "What do you mean, formerly?" My explanation that I was now non-practicing was obviously inadequate: he had typed me by various cues, and was confirmed in his hypothesis by my indication of ancestry. "You can always practice," he pursued, and I could only answer, "Anything is possible." It was an evasion at the time, but I later reflected that it was an assertion of freedom. We will never agree on my Jewishness, since he judges by ancestral legal standards and genealogy, whereas I join many of my contemporaries in making up my identity as I go along. The outcome of this disjunction between orthodox and secular Jews in Israel remains for the future, but there can be little doubt that in the United States people of a noncollective identity will multiply and prevail, stimulated as well as constrained by the complex associational claims on them. It would be premature to say that we are all cosmopolitans now, but there is hope that, following the vanguard of the New Class, we shall one day discover ourselves to be so.

NOTES

1. This is a major theme in William McNeill, *Polyethnicity and National Unity in World History* (Toronto, 1986).

2. In this brief summary of complicated and thoroughly researched developments in immigration history, I follow the standard works by Oscar Handlin, John Higham, and others, while omitting the substantial qualifications required by a survey of ethnicity that would include African- and Latin-American experiences.

3. In setting up this dichotomy, I avoid but do not ignore the tangled history of cultural pluralisms and their metaphors, well traced in Philip Gleason, *Speaking of Diversity: Language and Ethnicity in Twentieth-Century America* (Baltimore and London, 1992). Although the variety reflects real changes in social history and ideology, its deep structure may be visible in the polar statements summarized here.

4. The term "unmeltable ethnics" is the title of a text with this burden by Michael Novak, subtitled *Politics and Culture in American Life* (New Brunswick, N.J., and London, 1996 [1972]). The sociological awareness of enduring ethnic distinctness and its political expression was furthered by Nathan Glazer and Daniel P. Moynihan's *Beyond the Melting Pot: The Negroes, Puerto Ricans, Jews, Italians and Irish of New York City* (Cambridge, Mass., 1964).

5. Horace M. Kallen, *Cultural Pluralism and the American Idea: An Essay in Social Philosophy* (Philadelphia, 1956); quotations that follow are from pp. 53 and 98.

6. The results of regarding cultures as composed of units that can be detached to produce a desirable sum total may be seen in Stanford University's required "Culture, Ideas and Values" (CIV) program. The variety of courses offered to promote awareness of non-Western cultures allows each student access to a smorgasbord, each making a sampling according to taste. The offerings favor, moreover, currently assertive ethnic works over the great books of great civilizations: thus *The Tale of Genji, Dream of the Red Chamber*, and *Shakuntala* are less in evidence than Toni Morrison's *Beloved* and the mantras of Chief Seattle (not to speak of the fraudulent *I . . . Rigoberta Menchu*). See David O. Sacks and Peter A. Thiel, *The Diversity Myth: "Multiculturalism" and the Politics of Intolerance at Stanford* (Oakland, 1995), especially pp. 4–6; the entire book is instructive on the academic politics of cultural pluralism.

7. Frequently reprinted; I quote David A. Hollinger and Charles Capper, eds., *The American Intellectual Tradition: A Sourcebook* (New York and Oxford, 1993 [1989]), vol. 2; citations that follow are parenthetical.

8. In the current intellectual climate, the Columbia program has become the favored whipping boy of New Historians eager to expose the post–World War I, Western-culture educational programs as mere ideological window-dressing for expansive capitalism; see, for example, William V. Spanos, *The End of Education: Toward Posthumanism* (Minneapolis and London, 1993).

9. A brief recapitulation of relationships among these terms may be in order. I understand the New Class to consist of highly educated and well-rewarded

people generating or applying digitalized information; some but not all members of this class serve in the intelligentsia, consisting of clergy, academics, journalists, and others promulgating general ideas as well as specific data. I also understand intellectuals to represent a portion of the intelligentsia, those who originate or make striking formulations of ideas that the larger group promulgates in society.

10. See Marjorie Perloff, "Cultural Liminality/Aesthetic Closure? The 'Interstitial Perspective' of Homi Bhabha," *Literary Imagination* 1 (1999), 109–125, for an incisive critique of Bhabha's *Location of Culture* and his edited volume, *Nation and Narration*. For a more professional anthropological account of cultural interactions that produce complex new unities, see James L. Clifford's much cited essay, "Travelling Cultures," in Lawrence Grossberg et al., eds., *Cultural Studies: Now and in the Future* (New York, 1992).

11. Another instance of the cosmopolitan artist's endemic difficulties, even in a world that confers on him a Nobel Prize, is V.S. Naipaul's career. By origin a Trinidadian of Hindu immigrant descent but long an English resident, Naipaul has written scathingly both of the Caribbean as an "overcrowded barracoon" and of India as a "wounded civilization," thereby incurring wrath among all parties to his hybrid existence. He has also written imaginatively and movingly, in *The Enigma of Arrival*, from the detached yet incisive perspective acquired in becoming something like an English country gentleman.

12. Julia Kristeva, *Nations Without Nationalism*, Leon S. Roudiez, trans. (New York, 1993 [1990]). As a true postmodernist, Kristeva erects firm requirements for recognizing the value of otherness in others, but bases them on the otherness within oneself: "only strangeness is universal" (p. 21)—or as one wag inverts a classic formula, "everything alien is human to me."

13. For an application of Nussbaum's balance of universal and local norms to the American scene, see *Cultivating Humanity: A Classical Defense of Reform in Liberal Education* (Cambridge, Mass., and London, 1997).

14. Hannah Arendt, *The Origins of Totalitarianism*, part 2: Imperialism (New York, 1968 [1966]), pp. 115–116.

15. Lacking an insider's grasp of the terminology and assumptions of neo-Marxist theory, I rely on a summary of Balibar's views included in a useful survey by Amanda Anderson, "Cosmopolitanism, Universalism, and the Divided Legacies of Modernity," in Pheng Cheah and Bruce Robbins, eds., *Cosmopolitics: Thinking and Feeling Beyond Nationalism* (Minneapolis, 1998).

16. The title of a text by Michael Hardt and Antonio Negri that's "definitely hot" on campuses, according to a *New York Times* report (July 7, 2001).

17. Timothy Brennan, *At Home in the World: Cosmopolitanism Now* (Cambridge, Mass., 1997).

18. David Simpson, *Academic Postmodernism and the Rule of Literature: A Report on Half-Knowledge* (Chicago and London, 1995), p. 118.

19. A striking exception to this generalization is the career of Immanuel Wallerstein, an early theorist and bitter critic of the global economy; his current assessment and futuristic predictions are set out in *After Liberalism* (New York, 1995).

20. Bruce Robbins, *Secular Vocations: Intellectuals, Professionalism, Culture* (London and New York, 1993), p. 11.

21. See James Chatters, *Ancient Encounters: Kennewick Man and the First Americans* (New York, 2001), especially pp. 172–173.

22. Arendt, *The Origins of Totalitarianism*, part 2, p. 180.

23. John Higham, *Send These to Me: Immigrants in Urban America* (Baltimore and London, 1984 [1975]), p. 213.

24. Thomas M. Franck, *The Empowered Self: Law and Society in the Age of Individualism* (Oxford and New York, 1999), p. 10; quotations that follow are from pp. 59, 60, and 63.

25. David A. Hollinger, *Postethnic America: Beyond Multiculturalism* (New York, 1995); citations that follow are parenthetical. Hollinger has enlarged on this intellectual tradition in "Ethnic Diversity, Cosmopolitanism and the Emergence of the American Liberal Intelligentsia," in *In the American Grain: Studies in the History and Historiography of Ideas* (Bloomington, Ind., 1985), pp. 56–73.

26. Jeremy Waldron, "Minority Cultures and the Cosmopolitan Alternative," *University of Michigan Journal of Law Reform* 25 (1992), pp. 754–755; citations in text are parenthetical.

Select Bibliography

ON AMERICAN CULTURAL HISTORY

Conn, Steven. *Museums and American Intellectual Life, 1876–1926*. Chicago and London, 1998.

Douglas, Ann. *Terrible Honesty: Mongrel Manhattan in the 1920s*. New York, 1995.

Fuchs, Lawrence H. *The American Kaleidoscope: Race, Ethnicity, and the Civic Culture*. London and Hanover, N.H., 1990.

Haskell, Barbara. *The American Century: Art and Culture 1900–1950*. New York and London, 1999.

Hofstadter, Richard. *Anti-Intellectualism in American Life*. New York, 1963.

Hollinger, David A. and Charles Capper, eds. *The American Intellectual Tradition: A Sourcebook*. New York and Oxford, 1993 [1989].

Hughes, Robert. *American Visions: The Epic History of Art in America*. New York, 1999.

Kammen, Michael. *American Culture/American Tastes: Social Change and the 20th Century*. New York, 1999.

———. *Mystic Chords of Memory: The Transformation of Tradition in American Culture*. New York, 1991.

Levine, Lawrence W. *Highbrow/Lowbrow: The Emergence of Cultural Hierarchy in America*. Cambridge, Mass., and London, 1988.

Marx, Leo. *The Pilot and the Passenger: Essays on Literature, Technology and Culture in the United States*. New York and Oxford, 1988.

Michaels, Walter Benn. *Our America: Nativism, Modernism, and Pluralism*. Durham, N.C., and London, 1995.

Ziff, Larzer. *Literary Democracy: The Declaration of Cultural Independence in America*. New York, 1981.

ON CONTEMPORARY ARTS

Alexander, Paul. *Death and Disaster: The Rise of the Warhol Empire and the Race for Andy's Millions*. New York, 1994.

Bolton, Richard, ed. *Culture Wars: Documents from the Recent Controversies in the Arts*. New York, 1992.

Crane, Diana. *The Transformation of the Avant-Garde: The New York Art World 1940–85*. Chicago and London, 1987.

Gopnik, Adam and Kirk Varnedoe. *High and Low: Modern Art and Popular Culture*. New York, 1990.

Harrison, Charles, and Paul Wood, eds. *Art in Theory 1900–1990: An Anthology of Changing Ideas*. Oxford and Malden, Mass., 1992.

Herwitz, Daniel. *Making Theory/Constructing Art: On the Authority of the Avant-Garde*. Chicago and London, 1993.

Huyssen, Andreas. *After the Great Divide: Modernism, Mass Culture, Postmodernism*. Bloomington, Ind., and London, 1986.

Jameson, Fredric. *Postmodernism: Or, the Cultural Logic of Late Capitalism*. Durham, N.C., 1991.

Kuspit, Donald. *The New Subjectivism: Art in the 1980s*. Ann Arbor, Mich., and London, 1988.

Larson, Gary O. *American Canvas*. Washington, 1997.

Miller, Mark C. *Boxed In: The Culture of TV*. Evanston, Ill., 1988.

Mills, Nikolaus, ed. *Culture in an Age of Money: The Legacy of the 1980s in America*. Chicago, 1990.

Sandler, Irving. *Art of the Postmodern Era: From the Late 1960s to the Early 1990s*. New York, 1996.

Watson, Peter. *From Manet to Manhattan: The Rise of the Modern Art Market*. New York, 1992.

ON SOCIAL CLASS

Cannadine, David. *The Rise and Fall of Class in Britain*. New York, 1999.

DeMott, Benjamin. *The Imperial Middle: Why Americans Can't Think Straight about Class*. New York, 1990.

Fussell, Paul. *Caste Marks: Style and Status in the U.S.A.* London, 1984.

Kahlenberg, Richard D. *The Remedy: Class, Race, and Affirmative Action*. New York, 1996.

Kaus, Mickey. *The End of Equality*. New York, 1992.

Kingston, Paul W. *The Classless Society*. Stanford, Calif., 2000.

Marwick, Arthur. *Class in the Twentieth Century*. Brighton, U.K., 1986.

Taylor, Brian K., ed. *Race, Nation, Ethnos and Class: Quasi-Groups and Society*. Brighton, U.K., 1996.

Zweig, Mark. *The Working Class Majority: America's Best Kept Secret*. Ithaca, N.Y., and London, 2000.

ON THE NEW CLASS

Barry, John A. *Technobabble*. Cambridge, Mass., and London, 1991.

Bazelon, David T. *Power in America: The Politics of the New Class*. New York, 1967.

Bledstein, Burton J. *The Culture of Professionalism: The Middle Class and the Development of Higher Education in America*. New York, 1976.

Brint, Stephen. *In an Age of Experts: The Changing Role of Professionals in Politics and Public Life*. Princeton, N.J., 1994.

Brooks, David. *Bobos in Paradise: The New Upper Class and How They Got There*. New York, 2000.

Bruce-Briggs, B., ed. *The New Class?* New Brunswick, N.J., 1979.

Dery, Mark. *Escape Velocity: Cyberculture at the End of the Century*. New York, 1996.

Gouldner, Alvin W. *The Future of Intellectuals and the Rise of the New Class*. New York, 1979.

Heim, Michael. *The Metaphysics of Virtual Reality*. New York and Oxford, 1993.

Herrnstein, Richard J. and Charles Murray. *The Bell Curve: Intelligence and Class Structure in American Life*. New York, 1994.

Kellner, Hansfried and Frank W. Heuberger, eds. *Hidden Technocrats: The New Class and New Capitalism*. New Brunswick, N.J., and London, 1992.

Lasch, Christopher. *The Culture of Narcissism: American Life in an Age of Diminishing Expectations*. New York, 1978.

———. *The Revolt of the Elites and the Betrayal of Democracy*. New York and London, 1995.

Perkin, Harold. *The Rise of Professional Society: England since 1880*. London and New York, 1989.

Rawlins, Gregory J.E. *Moths to the Flame: The Seductions of Computer Technology*. Cambridge, Mass., and London, 1996.

Rheingold, Howard. *The Virtual Community: Homesteading on the Electronic Frontier*. Reading, Mass., 1993.

Turkle, Sherry. *Life on the Screen: Identity in the Age of the Internet*. New York, 1995.

Young, Michael. *The Rise of the Meritocracy: 1870–2033: An Essay on Education and Equality*. Baltimore, 1961 [1958].

ON COSMOPOLITANISM

Alba, Richard D. *Ethnic Identity: The Transformation of White America*. New Haven, Conn., and London, 1990.

Arendt, Hannah. *The Origins of Totalitarianism*. New York, 1968 [1966].

Bhabha, Homi K. *The Location of Culture*. New York and London, 1994.

Brennan, Timothy. *At Home in the World: Cosmopolitanism Now*. Cambridge, Mass., 1997.

Franck, Thomas M. *The Empowered Self: Law and Society in the Age of Individualism*. Oxford and New York, 1999.

Gleason, Philip. *Speaking of Diversity: Language and Ethnicity in Twentieth-Century America*. Baltimore and London, 1992.

Grossberg, Lawrence et al., eds. *Cultural Studies: Now and in the Future*. New York, 1992.

Higham, John. *Send These to Me: Immigrants in Urban America*. Baltimore and London, 1984 [1975].

Hollinger, David A. *Postethnic America: Beyond Multiculturalism*. New York, 1995.

Kallen, Horace. *Cultural Pluralism and the American Idea: An Essay in Social Phi-losophy*. Philadelphia, 1956.
Kristeva, Julia. *Nations Without Nationalism*. Leon S. Roudiez, trans. New York, 1993 [1990].
Lind, Michael. *The Next American Nation: The New Nationalism and the Fourth American Revolution*. New York, 1995.
McNeill, William. *Polyethnicity and National Unity in World History*. Toronto, 1986.
Robbins, Bruce. *Secular Vocations: Intellectuals, Professionalism, Culture*. London and New York, 1993.
Waldron, Jeremy. "Minority Cultures and the Cosmopolitan Alternative." *University of Michigan Journal of Law Reform* 25 (1992): 751–792.
Wallerstein, Immanuel. *After Liberalism*. New York, 1995.

ON THE SOCIOLOGY OF CULTURE

Alexander, Jeffrey C. *Fin de Siècle Social Theory: Relativism, Reduction, and the Problem of Reason*. London and New York, 1995.
Benedict, Stephen, ed. *Public Money and the Muse: Essays on Government Funding for the Arts*. New York and London, 1991.
Bourdieu, Pierre. *Distinction: A Social Critique of the Judgement of Taste*. Richard Nice, trans. Cambridge, Mass., 1984 [1979].
———. *The Field of Cultural Production: Essays on Art and Literature*. Randal Johnson, ed. New York, 1993.
———. *The Rules of Art: Genesis and Structure of the Literary Field*. Susan Emanuel, trans. Stanford, Calif., 1995 [1992].
Bradford, Gigi, Michael Gary, and Glenn Wallach, eds. *The Politics of Culture: Policy Perspectives for Individuals, Institutions, and Communities*. New York and Washington, 2000.
Bürger, Peter. *Theory of the Avant-Garde*. Michael Shaw and Jochen Schulte-Sasse, trans. Minneapolis, 1984 [1974].
Frith, Simon. *Performing Rites: On the Value of Popular Music*. Cambridge, Mass., 1996.
Gans, Herbert. *Popular Culture and High Culture: An Analysis and Evaluation of Taste*. New York, 1974.
Klamer, Arjo, ed. *The Value of Culture: On the Relationship between Economics and the Arts*. Amsterdam, 1996.
Shils, Edward. *The Intellectuals and the Powers and Other Essays*. Chicago and London, 1972.
Simpson, Charles R. *SoHo: The Artist and the City*. Chicago and London, 1981.
Swingewood, Alan. *The Myth of Mass Culture*. Atlantic Highlands, N.J., 1977.

Index

About the Author

AVROM FLEISHMAN is Professor Emeritus of English at Johns Hopkins University, where he taught graduate and undergraduate courses in Victorian and modern literature. He is the author of eight books, including *The Condition of English* (Greenwood, 1998).